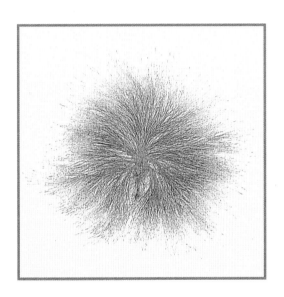

the Pressed Plant

CONVOLVVLVS foliis cordatis integris trilobisque, corollis indiuifis, fructibus erectis. *Linn. fpec.* 2. 219. *Ludw.* D. G. P. 105.
- - - - - - - hederaceus.

the Pressed Plant

THE ART OF
Botanical Specimens,
Nature Prints, and
Sun Pictures

Andrea DiNoto & David Winter
Photography by John Berens

stewart, tabori & chang
NEW YORK

A Note on Illustrations and Captions

Unless otherwise noted, all specimen and nature-print photographs are from the collection of David Winter. Captions reflect the plant names given in the item illustrated and are not necessarily botanically accurate.

Published in 1999 by
Stewart, Tabori & Chang
A division of U.S. Media Holdings, Inc.
115 West 18th Street
New York, NY 10011

Distributed in Canada by
General Publishing Company Ltd.
30 Lesmill Road
Don Mills, Ontario, Canada M3B 2T6

Library of Congress Cataloging-in-Publication Data

DiNoto, Andrea.
    The pressed plant : the art of botanical specimens, nature prints, and sun prints / by
Andrea DiNoto & David Winter ; photography by John Berens.
    p.   cm.
Includes bibliographic references.
ISBN 1- 55670-936-6
    1. Pressed flower pictures. 2. Plants—collection and preservation. I. Winter, David
(David L.), 1955–
SB449.3.P7D56 1999   99-16501
                                                           CIP

Edited by Marisa Bulzone
Design by Lisa Vaughn
Graphic Production by Kim Tyner

Printed and bound in Spain by Artes Gráficas Toledo, S.A.U.
D.L. TO: 1388 - 1999
The text of this book was composed in Adobe Garamond, Cenatur, Gaston, and Rotis Sans Serif

10 9 8 7 6 5 4 3 2 1

First Printing

For Agata, and for Flora Farnham, and in memory of Anne DiNoto

ACKNOWLEDGMENTS

We wish to thank the following people who assisted in the preparation of this book:

Lisa Hammel provided invaluable editorial suggestions and wrote portions of the text, including the section "Women in Botany" in its entirety. Linda Hetzer's Internet research formed the basis for the appendices.

Rick Dodge entrusted us with rare examples of botanical specimens of sea mosses. Philip Taaffe permitted us to photograph from nineteenth-century books on nature printing from his collection.

Hans P. Kraus, Jr. shared his extensive knowledge of early photography and provided important illustrations for that section of the text.

At the New York Public Library, Julia van Haaften, Curator of Photography Collections, supplied encouragement and facilitated access to Anna Atkins's material.

At the New York Botanical Garden Herbarium, director Patricia Holmgren permitted us to view and photograph a fascinating random sample of botanical specimens; Bee Gunn guided us through the herbarium and made useful suggestions. At the NYBG Library, director John Reed arranged for us to photograph several examples of rare nature prints from the library's collection.

Early on, John Waite helped lead us into the "heyday of natural history" and supplied our collections with several outstanding botanical specimens.

Eric Hochberg, Sonja Larsen, and Peter Heilmann contributed hard-to-find research materials relating to the history of nature printing.

Barbara Ertter of the Jepson Herbarium, Berkeley, shared information on current botanical activities.

Terry Ackerman helped research the plant hunters, supplied important leads to materials, and provided other editorial assistance. Linda Campbell Franklin contributed "Sunday" research and provided photographic materials from her archives.

John Berens, our friend and photographer, stood ever at the ready for "one last shoot."

Frank Farnham was our computer expert whose patience, wit, and understanding helped bring words to the page—and keep them there.

Thanks to Peter Kennedy and Nicholas Goodyer, who helped to build this collection.

Finally, we thank our agent, Martha Kaplan, for finding the perfect home for this book, and Marisa Bulzone, our editor at Stewart, Tabori & Chang, for her enthusiasm and wise guidance through the complexities of its realization.

Contents

Naturselbstdruck.
Aus der k. k. Hof- und Staatsdruckerei zu Wien. 1853.

appendices:

Genus *Nephrolepis*
Species *tuberosa*
Patria *B. Appini*
1851

preface: *the collection*

As a sculptor, I had long been interested in the geometry of natural forms. In the plant photographs of the early twentieth-century German artist and teacher Karl Blossfeldt, I had discovered riveting images that exposed this formal geometry with utter directness—and strangeness. Blossfeldt's magnified details of plants, which often suggest anthropomorphic or architectural forms, were stronger than anything I had seen in conventional botanical illustration. Later, when I stumbled upon botanical specimens, I recognized and was equally amazed by that same simplicity and directness.

I discovered botanical specimens for the first time, quite by accident, in 1992. I was at a preview of a general book auction at Swann Gallery in New York City where I was looking for prints by Piranesi and other artists whose work related to my sculptural interests. By chance, I opened an oversized leather-bound volume and was shocked to be looking at a real blade of grass. This was a herbarium, a collection of dried, pressed, and mounted plant specimens that in this instance had been bound in book form and published, complete with typeset captions. The illustrations were the plants themselves. I found that a blade of grass, flattened and isolated on the page, had

tremendous graphic power. Ironically, the space implied on the page was deeper than that around a living blade of grass in a field. This catalog of grasses, *Hortus Gramineus Woburnensis,* had been produced in 1816 by George Sinclair, gardener to the duke of Bedford, as a horticultural guide for farmers, but it had all the power of a book of art.

I bought the Sinclair at that auction and began my search for more specimens. Sometime later, at a print shop, I saw for the first time a few plates from an 1855 botanical classic, *Ferns of Great Britain and Ireland* by Thomas Moore with illustrations by Henry Bradbury. This was not a herbarium of actual plants; the images contained in it were made by pressing real ferns directly into a soft metal plate. When the pressings hardened, multiple images could be struck from the plate. The technique, called electrotype nature printing, produces an image that is a near-perfect replication, worm holes, broken bits, and all. Unlike most botanical illustration, which tends to idealize the plant, nature printing shocks us with its veracity.

Not until one drizzly day in London at the Portobello Road flea market did I first see a complete edition of the Bradbury Ferns, as the Moore volume is commonly called. I encountered a dealer who knew of the book and actually had a copy for sale. He also showed me a book illustrated by an eighteenth-century German printmaker named Heironymus Kniphhof.

opposite: Botanical specimen. *Nephrolepsis.* From a herbarium of Darjeeling ferns, 1882. 18 x 12 in.

Triticum caninum.

ʙ

Bearded Wheat-grass.

Kniphof used another, earlier, nature-printing method in which an image is made by inking the plant itself and pressing it directly to paper. I acquired both the Bradbury and Kniphof on the spot and started what was to become a comprehensive collection of both specimens and nature prints. Soon the collection expanded to include botanical photograms, images made by placing plants on photo-sensitive paper and exposing them to sunlight.

When I met Andrea DiNoto in 1997, her enthusiasm for this material led to our collaboration on the book at hand. We believe it is the first to bring together

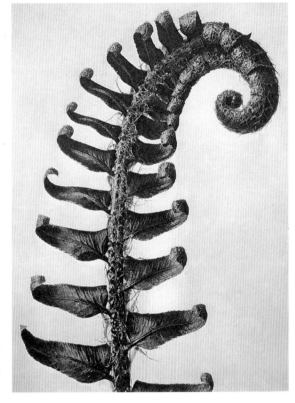

these diverse yet related botanical images, all of which are, or have been made from, actual plants. Although a small number of people have been putting collections together, some for more than twenty years, the related fields of botanical specimens, nature prints, and photograms remain relatively unexplored. Only one comprehensive book in English, Cave and Wakeman's *Typographia Naturalis*, has been written on the history of nature printing, although several hobbyist books

exist that describe the various techniques used in their creation. Outside of botanical textbooks, little has been written on botanical specimens per se. Until now, specimens have been considered strictly as scientific tools, a form of evidential record-keeping that has been the backbone of botanical science for more than two hundred years.

Literally millions of specimens fill the herbarium cabinets of each of the world's great botanical gardens. The romance of botanical collecting—stories of intrepid botanists seeking rare plants in the wilderness—is only one part of this subject's colorful history. We present these specimens to be appreciated in their own right; as art, if you will, created quite inadvertently by both scientists and enthusiasts of nature unadorned. We present them, together with nature prints and photograms, commonly called sun pictures, as an homage to the plant itself.

David Winter
Andrea DiNoto
New York 1999

above: Rotogravure. Karl Blossfeldt, 1928. *Polystichum munitum.* Shield-fern. Young rolled-up frond enlarged almost 5½ times.

opposite: Botanical specimen. Bearded wheat grass used as an illustration in *Gramineus Wobornensis* by George Sinclair, 1816. Page size: 19¼ x 12 in.

introduction:
botanical art, from jurassic lilies to sun pictures

A cursory glance through this book might lead one to think that the images are drawings or paintings. In fact, with the exception of those shown in this introduction, they are either *real* pressed plants (known as botanical specimens) or images made directly from plants themselves. Together they constitute intriguing footnotes to the larger, but related subjects of botanical art and illustration. The unique beauty of pressed plants makes them easily appreciated as aesthetic objects as well, yet they are best viewed in the context of botanical illustration, a handmaiden to the science of botany.

Both botanical art and botanical specimens are concerned with the documentation of plants. From earliest times, artists have depicted plants with passionate dedication and with amazing range—from Egyptian bas-reliefs to crude medieval woodcuts to sumptuous nineteenth-century watercolors.

Nature itself created the earliest images of actual plants. Fossils, millions of years old, hold detailed images, often with stems, leaves, petals, and even insect life captured and preserved over eons. These are the original nature prints from which paleobotanists chart the rise of plant life on earth. It was not until centuries after the rise of agriculture that plants are found drawn by human hands. The cave paintings of Lascaux, France, and other sites of celebrated prehistoric art depict mainly animals, although examples of aboriginal rock art in Australia bear imprints of grasses (Hochberg 1985).

One of the earliest renderings of plant forms is an Egyptian stone relief of germinating seedlings that was carved on the walls of the Great Temple of Thutmose III at Karnak around 1450 B.C. By that time, the domestication of plants as sources of food, medicines, and adornments for ornamental gardens was well established. Egyptian archaeology tells us that when flax was a staple crop, anemones, narcissi, and lilies grew in the gardens of the Pharaohs. There are hieroglyphic names for 202 kinds of plants. The interest in collecting plants was such that in 1495 B.C. Queen Hatshepsut sent plant hunters from Thebes to a land called Punt (which may be present-day Somalia) in search of myrrh trees. Thirty-one living specimens were brought back and planted (Blunt 1967).

Several thousand years earlier than the Egyptians, however, the Chinese were engaged in extensive medical botany, which was codified between A.D. 1560 and 1590 in the great pharmacopoeia Pun-tsao. Extensive Chinese gardens, in which many flowers—including rambler roses, chrysanthemums, and poppies—were cultivated were described as early as 206 B.C. and eventually brought to the West.

In the third century B.C., the Greek writer Theophrastus, who was called the father of botany and had been a pupil of Aristotle's, produced *Historia Plantarum* (Inquiry into Plants). This was considered the first attempt to classify plants—medicinal, ornamental, and aquatic—and describe their parts and uses. Much of the information was based on Theophrastus's own observations, but the treatise also included reports from observers who had accompanied Alexander the Great into Persia and India during the Persian wars. The tamarind and coconut from India, the banana ("having leaves two cubits long, like ostrich feathers") probably from Assyria, the yellow Persian rose, and the Lombardy poplar were among Alexander's botanical trophies (Whittle 1997, 18).

In Rome, around the middle of the first century A.D., Pliny the Elder included botany in his thirty-seven volume *Historia Naturalis.* But for fifteen centuries, the definitive botanical text was the five-volume *De Materia Medica* by the first century A.D.

Fossil. *Seirocrinus subangularis.* Extinct Jurassic sea lily, 190 million years old. Posidonienschiefer formation, Holzmaden, Germany. 63 x 31½. Courtesy of Phillips Gallery, New York.

Greek physician Pedanius Dioscorides. A magnificent, illustrated copy of Dioscorides's work dating from A.D. 512, known as the *Codex Vindobonensis* and now a treasure of the National Library, Vienna, Austria, describes about six hundred different kinds of medicinal plants. Blunt calls it a "magnificent manuscript" that "displays a standard of excellence in plant drawing that was not to be surpassed for almost a thousand years" (10). The naturalistic watercolor drawings in the codex (the artist is unknown) inspired generations of copyists across the civilized world, but the continued copying of this and other herbals led to a decline in the quality of botanical art through the end of the fourteenth century[1]

---

[1] The quality of botanical writing and thinking was advanced, however, in the thirteenth century by the Dominican monk Albertus Magnus, whose *De Vegetabilibus* is considered "the most important theoretical treatise on plants since Theophrastus" (Greene 1983, I: 448). It is also notable for its precise observations of plants, such as the alder, which is described in part as "a tree that loves moist spots. Its wood is reddish, covered by a brown and rather smooth bark and yields a perfectly white ash. It grows in ring-like layers of wood: when dry it splits more readily than Pine and it can be preserved under water for centuries. The leaves of the Alder are rounded like those of the Pear, but are not so hard and of a darker green" (Hawks 1928, 106).

Only in the Far East, Blunt notes (161), did reverence for and courtesy[2] toward nature foster a consistent approach to botanical art that displays a highly refined sense of design, values empathy with the subject, and produces economy of line emphasizing the plant's dynamic form.

By the late Middle Ages and into the early Renaissance, a renewed interest in the beauty and scientific aspects of the natural world inspired artists to fill paintings, carvings, tapestries, and illuminated manuscripts and miniatures with a teeming world of colorful plant and animal life, all rendered with astonishing realism. Among the most glorious examples are the illuminated manuscripts called Books of Hours (used for prayer and meditation) especially those produced in fourteenth-century Burgundy. In Venice in the late fourteenth and early fifteenth centuries, three important illustrated herbals were produced, the most notable of which is a circa 1415 manuscript by Benedetto Rinio with more than five hundred full-page paintings of plants by one Andrea Amadio, who drew plants with remarkable realism and in vivid opaque color (Blunt, 26–27).

Although botanically accurate renditions of plants began to appear in the landscapes of the Florentine painters, few true botanical studies exist by early Renaissance painters, outside of sketches by Pisanello, Jacopo Bellini, and Leonardo da Vinci, and the extraordinary woodcuts and paintings of Albrecht Dürer.

In a class of their own are the peerless Dutch flower paintings produced in the sixteenth and seventeenth centuries, which, though outside the tradition of scientific botany, are among the glories of horticultural art. They represent an expanded interest in plants from the strictly medicinal to the decorative. These paintings virtually brought indoors flower gardens filled with ravishing colors and exotic fragrance. Plants were painted with as much care and naturalism as the documentation of beneficial herbs. Among the rarest and most costly blossoms painted by the Dutch artists were tulips, newly imported from the Far East, that caused a craze known as Tulipomania.[3] Legend has it that Dutch flower paintings now considered masterpieces were sometimes commissioned by people who could not afford to buy the actual flowers.

With the development of printing in the fifteenth and sixteenth centuries, several herbals based upon Dioscorides's *De Materia Medica* (although including considerably fewer plants) were produced with

---

[2] In a Japanese poem, a young girl who goes to fetch water from a well finds that a morning-glory vine has grown around the bucket's cord. Respecting the plant, she seeks water elsewhere (Blunt, 161).

[3] During the Tulipomania craze that reached its peak from 1633–37 in Holland, rare bulbs, imported from Turkey during that era, were traded in the manner of stock by market speculators. By 1610, a single bulb was considered an acceptable dowry; in France an entire brewery was exchanged for one bulb of the variety *Tulipe brasserie*. Prices surged to unimaginable heights in the 1630s, as traders mortgaged homes and estates to buy bulbs for resale and profit. Fortunes were lost in what was considered a national scandal.

woodcut illustrations that, while recognizably portraying the plant, rendered it in a simplified, stylized manner.[4] Not until the great 1530 *Herbarum Vivae Eicones* (Living Portraits of Plants), compiled by the German physician and botanist Otto Brunfels, with illustrations by Hans Weiditz, did the woodcut reach a high level of artistry. Plants in this volume appeared to have been drawn from life with great specificity and vivacity, but its achievement was rare among a plethora of herbals that more or less copied one another, resulting in uninspired, somewhat crude artwork.

But, as the woodcut declined, the arts of engraving and etching developed and flourished from the early sixteenth century onward. In 1613, the immense two-volume florilegium *Hortus Eystettensis*, the Nuremberg Apothecary of Basil Besler illustrated a thousand flowers and 667 species organized by seasons: it remained the definitive botanical reference with unrivaled art for two centuries. The Besler, as it is commonly known, illustrated with 374 engraved plates and published in

Five Tulips. *Tulipa lutea maculis aspersa minutis* and friends. Hand-colored engraved plate from *Hortus Eystettensis* by Basil Besler, 1613. Courtesy of Swann Galleries.

Eichstütt, near Nuremberg, Germany, is considered horticultural rather than botanical because it describes cultivated flowers in a single garden, that of a German nobleman. This horticultural direction was taken up in the eighteenth century by the German-born botanical illustrator George Dionysius Ehret, who lived most of his life in England where he painted garden plants of the duchess of Portland, among other subjects. A few color plates of Ehret's great flower illustrations are included in *The Natural History of Carolina, Florida, and the Bahama Islands*, a landmark book of eighteenth-century American flora and fauna compiled by the English naturalist Mark Catesby.

In England in the first half of the nineteenth century botanical art was dominated by John Thornton's *Temple of Flora*, an extravagant flower book of twenty-eight paintings by several artists. Each is accompanied by an appropriately florid text[5] by Thornton, a physician turned-botanist, who was ruined financially by his all-consuming project. In France,

---

[4] The British artist and nonsense poet Edward Lear would spoof such herbals, with their arcane botanical Latin names, in his 1871 *Nonsense Botany*, which included such drawings as a plant labeled "Manypeeplia Upsidownia" (Blunt, 41).

[5] Thorton's white lily "majestically presents its finely-polished bosom to the all enlivening sun" (Blunt, 207).

the Belgian-born Pierre Joseph Redouté, certainly the most celebrated botanical artist of all time, produced several now-famous portfolios of flowers, including irises and lilacs, in watercolors and hand-colored stippled engravings. But it is Redouté's exquisite renderings of roses from the garden of Josephine Bonaparte, painted under her patronage, that occupy the most highly favored niche in the annals of the genre, and are especially prized in interior decoration.

Redouté may well mark the end of the golden age of botanical illustration. Twentieth-century illustrators have produced interesting work in all media, but the art form has become largely recreational. Art photography, however, has introduced an important new dimension in the depiction of plants, from Blossfeldt's strange, microscopic monochrome enlargements to Edward Steichen's lush color photos of the délphiniums he cultivated in his garden in the 1930s and 1940s to the stylized contemporary photographs of John Stezaker, a conceptual artist who based a series of images on the art of Redouté. But, like much botanical art, these are only marginally related to scientific illustration.

Throughout this long history, the plant specimen has been regarded primarily as a record of a species available to the illustrator as a model to draw from in every season. Nature printing, with which Leonardo da Vinci experimented in the fifteenth century, made various disparate appearances during the eighteenth and nineteenth centuries as a handy and economical method by which botanists, unskilled at sketching or unable to mount and store specimens, could create

plant collections. Nature-printed books and even currency—demonstrating the versatility of a technique that would flower in the mid-nineteenth century as a printing phenomenon—later receded into arcane realms, leaving botanical illustration to continue its evolution in the hands of specialist illustrators. The early nineteenth-century photograms, or sun pictures, of Fox Talbot and Anna Atkins remain technical curiosities, although they are also intimations of art photography to come.

From the outset, botanical art was married to botanical science, never more faithfully than during the great age of Colonial expansion, which began in the sixteenth century and peaked in the mid-nineteenth century at the time of the publication of Charles Darwin's *On the Origin of Species* (1849). The gathering of plant specimens was critical to mapping the seemingly limitless realms of what was commonly called "the vegetable kingdom." The task was performed often in uncharted territories by intrepid botanists—male and female—many of whom were dedicated amateurs studiously combing landscapes, familiar and otherwise, for rare or unknown species. Specimens gathered by these horticultural pioneers today furnish the vast herbariums, or plant libraries, at the world's great botanical gardens. The majority of specimens shown in this book are American and British exemplars that have been passed down through generations and have come to light in estate sales and through antiques and rare book and print dealers. In a time of virtual realities, we are stunned by their tangible beauty.

opposite top: Pierre Joseph Redouté. *Iris de Lemmonier.* Hand-colored lithograph of yellow irises from Redouté's *Les Liliacées,* Paris, 1802–16. Courtesy of Swann Galleries.

opposite bottom: Robert Thornton. *Large Flowering Sensitive Plant.* Hand-finished color aquatint and stipple print from *The Temple of Flora,* London, 1801. Courtesy of Swann Galleries.

Aralia Spikenard Wild Sarsaparilla
Aralia nudicaulis.
Wild Sarsaparilla.
Gray

Class V. Pentandria
Order II. Pentagynia
Aralia nudicaulis
Wild Sarsaparilla Bigelow.

A. P. J.

the plant

collected

The word botany conveys an idyllic Victorian

past in which genteel ladies, well-behaved children, and earnest clergy gath-

ered plants as a scholarly pursuit for a Sunday afternoon. There is some truth

to that vision, as we shall see, but the larger story of botany embraces science,

adventure, and exploration, the goal of which was the pursuit and collection

of plants the world over.

opposite: Botanical specimen. Spikenard and wild sarsaparilla, 1880s. 17½ x 11½ in. Collection of Andrea DiNoto.

botanical
specimens

"The organic form . . . is innate; it shapes as it develops itself from within, and the fullness of its development is one and the same with the perfection of its outward form."

—*Samuel Taylor Coleridge*

Botanical specimen. Common lyre-leaved sage.
Lambertville, New Jersey, 1883. 12 x 9½ in.

A REAL PLANT that has been pressed, dried, and mounted within the frame of a page assumes the guise of a drawing and persuades us to consider it as art. It is inspiring, of course, but it is not art. It is a botanical specimen, an artifact of the natural world. Specimens probably have been collected since antiquity, but most examples date from the nineteenth and early twentieth centuries. There is a curious poetic justice in that the majority of these specimens are now considered "works on paper," to be found today among the treasures in the stocks of rare book and print dealers and at natural history book auctions.[6]

Specimens, like fossils, become their own unique art form: illustrations, abstractions, essences of themselves; quasi-scientific

---

[6] Millions of well-documented specimens are stored, for the purposes of botanical study, at each of the world's great botanical gardens, such as Kew, in England, and the New York Botanical Garden. In these institutions, specimens comprise huge libraries of pressed and mounted plants, called herbariums. The same term is used to describe any collection of specimens, regardless of size.

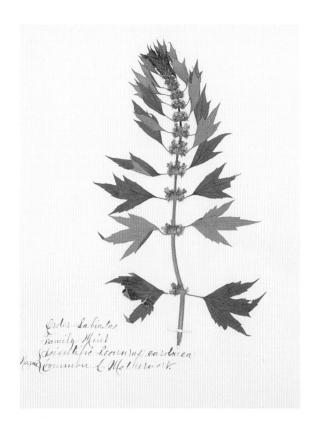

top row: Botanical specimens. Lambertville, New Jersey, 1883. left: Common beard tongue; right: Common mother wort. Each 12 x 9½ in. bottom row: Botanical specimens, all collected in Italy, from a grand tour herbarium. left: Ivy from a Capuchin monastery, Naples; right, top: Olive leaves from Fiesole; right, bottom: unidentified flower from Tivoli.

"Rose of Sharon"
South of the
Lebanon

Lily of the field
Matt 6:28
Lebanon

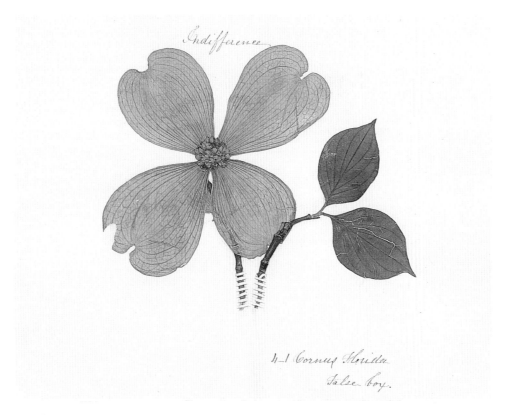

Indifference

*4—1 Cornus florida.
False box.*

Botanical specimen. *Cornus florida.* American eastern dogwood, nineteenth century.
Inscribed "Indifference." 10 x 8 in.

documents that time has turned into artifacts, whose mysterious beauty is also linked to their powers of survival. They are amazingly durable, from fibrous stems to diaphanous petals, and the fact that they have lasted so long—sometimes two-hundred years—owes little or nothing to technology. That they have survived at all is due to lucky circumstance—a credit to the competence of the person who mounted them, and of having been stored safe from damaging moisture and marauding insects. In many cases, even the vegetal colors, though muted through fading, have survived, exquisitely subtle, even poignant in their delicacy. In short, any artistic quality they seem to possess is the result of

a felicitous accident, the coming together of a plant with a person who simply shows it in its optimal detail and simplicity.

The specimens in this book demonstrate the two forms in which they are commonly found: single sheets, which can be part of extensive multisheet portfolios, and bound sheets. Whether loose-leaf or bound, any organized collection of specimens is properly called a herbarium. Bound herbaria can be of almost any type. Some have cardboard covers—the equivalent of a scrapbook or album; some are spiral-bound notebooks preprinted expressly for the purpose; and some have elegant gold-stamped leather bindings. Whatever the binding, it is the quality of the specimens within that is of greatest interest and importance.

A herbarium can be a miscellany of plants or it can focus on one particular type—grasses, for

opposite: Botanical specimen. Nettles with silk ribbon. Biblical herbarium, nineteenth century.
preceding pages: Botanical specimens from a Biblical herbarium, souvenir of the Holy Land, nineteenth century. left: Rose of sharon; right: Lily of the field.

Washington
died
Nov.ʳ 15ᵗʰ 1799.

Victorian-era composed
seaweed pictures. top right and left:
Arrangements resembling drawings; bottom: A fanciful
image inscribed "The
Mermaid's Dog."

opposite: George Washington's
tomb, rendered in various
seaweeds, with obelisk and
weeping willows. 6½ x 5¼ in.
Collection of Rick Dodge.

instance, or ferns; or on plants from a particular geographic area. One especially charming type of herbaria is the Victorian-era grand tour souvenir. Many of these were made by individuals, but many more were produced commercially and sold to tourists in favored locales such as Italy, the Holy Land, or the Swiss Alps. The presence of typeset specimen labels and unusual packaging, such as a boxed collection of alpine flowers, for example, suggests that it had been professionally prepared.

Specimens were also used artfully to create decorative collage pictures made from bits and pieces of plants or seaweed. Some are simple and sentimental, others are elaborate multimedia Victorian collages. More akin to decorative art, they are skillfully and painstakingly constructed and ornately framed.

Real Plants on Printed Pages

The most sophisticated form of herbarium is the printed agricultural text that uses actual dried specimens as illustrations, as shown opposite and on pages 30 and 31. This feat of publishing, in which each of hundreds of specimens were mounted by hand on printed pages, probably occurred first in the early to mid-nineteenth century. Written by and for gardeners, they were usually published through the patronage of a wealthy landowner. One such example is the *Hortus Gramineus Woburnensis*, an oversized volume published in London in 1816 by B. McMillan that was, as the subtitle states, "an account of the results of experiments on the produce and nutritive qualities of different grasses and other plants, used as the food of the

more valuable domestic animals." Written by George Sinclair, gardener to the duke of Bedford, the *Hortus* offered "practical observations on natural habit [of the grasses], and the soils best adapted to their growth."

Specimens of grasses, such as the striped reed canary-grass (*Arundo colorata*), are affixed by means of printed labels to the pages, with text descriptions and observations opposite. The shock of the real upon opening such a book is profound, especially as the specimens are not only in perfect condition but in most cases flowering and with their subtle natural colorations (although color is added in some instances). Page after page of the slender, pressed reedlike grasses inspire awe and even reverence, not only for the care it must have taken to accomplish such a project but for the sheer beauty of the plants.

Just how difficult it was to produce these books is described in the preface to another such text, *Natural Illustrations of the British Grasses*, published in 1846:

Natural illustrations in botany, or dried specimens of plants, when preserved with care as to their natural appearance and character, must always be more interesting and valuable to a botanist, or a lover of nature, than engravings; being the real or original object, which drawings are intended only to pourtray [sic]. It was principally with this conviction that the present undertaking was attempted; the editor considering such a series of Specimens of British Grasses to be a desideratum, and at least more natural, if not more useful than any engravings, however excellent; for it will be allowed that there is an immeasurable distance between the most exquisite work of Art and that of Nature, inasmuch as the one is perfect and the other imperfect...there

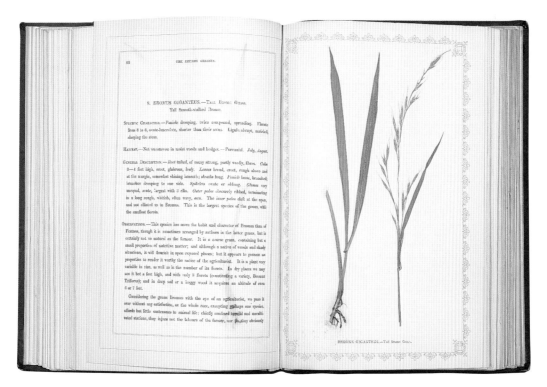

Real grass plants, such as *Bromus giganteus,* shown above, were hand-mounted throughout *Natural Illustrations of the British Grasses,* published in 1846. Page size 12½ x 16 in.

is much, in even the simplest production of the earth, that the pencil can never show.

It can be imagined that there were considerable difficulties:

The Editor would simply call attention of the reader to the great difficulties and labour attending [the] execution, when it is considered that the edition of this work requires no less than 62,000 plants to be collected and prepared [for an edition of 1,000]; in addition perhaps to at least half as many more culled to obtain that number of successful specimens. [Further,] collector has had to contend with every adverse circumstance of weather; and the scarceness of some of the species rendering it necessary to extend his researches to a considerable distance. Add to this, the brevity of the season in which all these were to be collected and prepared; and lastly, though not least, the difficulty [in] preventing any of the species being erroneously named, or misplaced, in the collection and preparation of so great a number.[7]

[7] Such books were not the first examples of real-plant illustration. Schama (1996, 19) relates the story of the *xylotheque,* or wooden library, the "product of a time when scientific inquiry and poetical sensibility seemed effortlessly and wittily married: the Enlightenment of the eighteenth century. In the German culture where modern forestry began, some enthusiast thought to go one better than the botanical volumes that merely illustrated the taxonomy of trees. Instead the books themselves were to be fabricated from their subject matter, so that the volume on *Fagus,* for example, the common European beech, would be bound in the bark of that tree. Its interior would contain samples of beech nuts and seeds; and its pages would literally be its leaves, the folios its *feuilles.* But the wooden books were not pure caprice, a nice pun on the meaning of cultivation. By paying homage to the vegetable matter from which it, and all literature, was constituted, the wooden library made a dazzling statement about the necessary union of culture and nature."

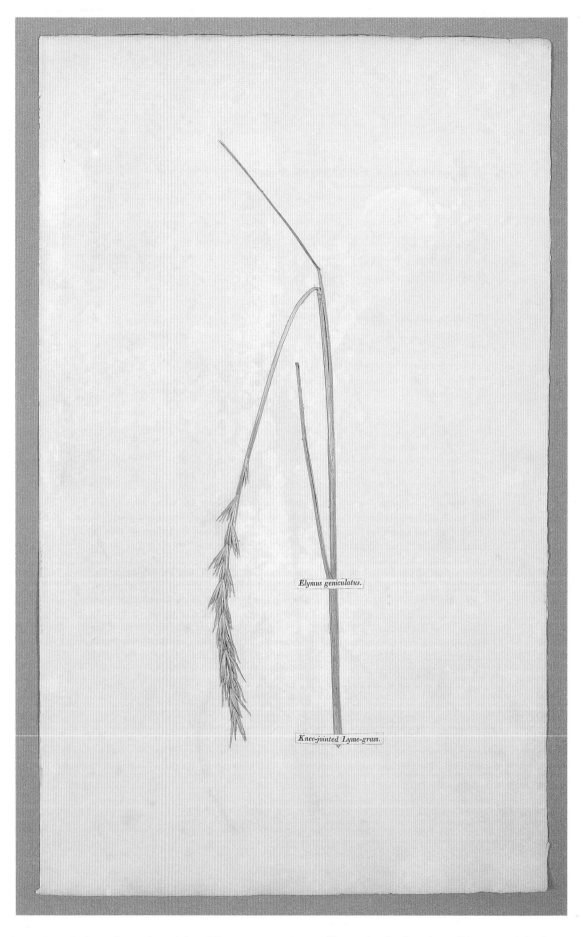

Elymus geniculatus.

Knee-jointed Lyme-grass.

above: Botanical specimen. Knee-jointed lime-grass used as an illustration in *Gramineus Wobornensis* by George Sinclair, 1816. Page size: 19¼ x 12 in. opposite: Botanical specimen. Barren bromegrass used as an illustration in *Gramineus Wobornensis* by George Sinclair, 1816. Page size: 19¼ x 12 in.

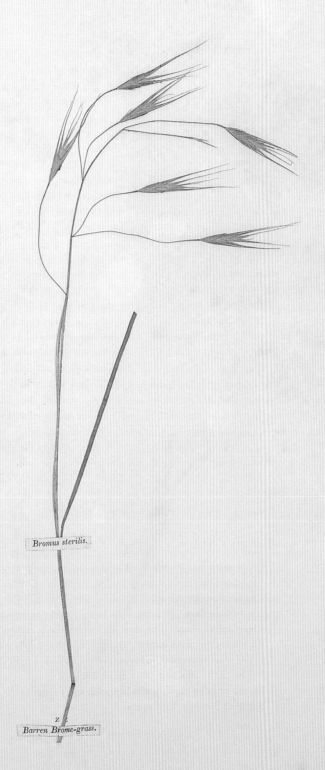

Bromus sterilis.

z z
Barren Brome-grass.

for every plant, two names:
the legacy of carolus linnaeus

Apart from its common name, every plant has a two-part Latin botanical name that places it definitively within the greater plant kingdom. Peppermint, for example, is properly called *Mentha piperita*, which shows that it belongs to the genus (general group) *Mentha*, and species (a group with similar characteristics) *piperita*. But plant names were not always so easy to decipher. By the eighteenth century, many plants had acquired long, impossibly complex names that could vary from country to country or from one botanist to another. Peppermint, for example, was once written *Mentha floribus capitatus, foliis lanceolatis serratis subpetiolatis.* Clearly, a method was needed for standardizing terminology.

In the late seventeenth and early eighteenth centuries, several botanists began to work entirely on taxonomy, in this case a system of naming and classifying organisms. In England, John Ray divided flowering plants into two main groups that emphasized their natural relationship. In France, J. P. de Tournefort was the

first to clearly define and characterize genera, groups of plants with certain similarities.

But the greatest taxonomic advance was made in the eighteenth century when the Swedish naturalist Carolus Linnaeus devised the first universal system for naming organisms. Linnaeus stated that "botany has a double basis: classification...and nomenclature." Classification has to do with plant structure; nomenclature with identification of genus and species. It is the latter, his binomial (two-name) system of nomenclature, that is his greatest legacy: it is considered the foundation of modern taxonomy. He published this system in 1753 as *Species Plantarum,* in which he gives Latin binomials to 7,300 plants. (He also gave himself the Latin binomial Carolus Linnaeus, based on his given Swedish name of Carl von Linné.)

The species name is sometimes the name of a plant's discoverer or a name that honors a particular person. The binomal is also found with the discoverer's name appended to it. Plants that were first described by Linnaeus have the letter L. after the binomial (*Mentha piperita L.*). Linnaeus also devised a system that organized flowering plants into twenty-three classes, according to the number of male reproductive organs, or stamens. These were named *monandria* (one man), *diandria* (two men), and so forth, through *polyandria* (many men). He then subdivided the (male) classes into orders based on the female organs, or pistils. The orders

PETANDRIA DIGYNIA.

Angelica sylvestris.

Ang: Angelica —.

—— Marshy places, & damp woods— July, Sept.——

It is warm & aromatic, but the cultivated kind possessing these properties in a much higher degree this plant has been neglected —

An eighteenth-century botanical caption reflects the Linnaean binomial system of plant naming.

were named sequentially *monogynia* (one woman), *digynia* (two women), *trigynia,* and so forth. The result was that a lilac, for example, would have the class/order designation *Diandria* (two stamens) *monogynia* (one pistil). The flowerless plants—ferns, fungi, and mosses—were grouped together in the twenty-fourth class under the heading *Cryptogamia,* "hidden sex." In describing the process by which plants self-fertilize, Linnaeus spoke in unabashed, yea scandalous, metaphor. *Polyandria* he described as "twenty males or more in the same bed with

the female," then proceeded into explicitness that engendered accusations of "loathesome harlotry" and "gross purience." However, botanists, both professional and amateur alike, enthusiastically adopted this method of classification because it was simple to learn. As a result, old botanical specimens are often found labeled with Linnaean binomials. Linnaeus's sexual classification system is considered "artificial" because it groups organisms by only one type of criteria. It has fallen into disuse for two main reasons: first, because it often results in odd bedfellows. The very dissimilar cherry and cactus, for example, which have the same number of stamens, fall into the same class; second, because the system is unrelated to evolutionary, or phylogenetic, history. Linnaeus, of course, knew nothing of Darwin's Theory of Evolution, as he lived a hundred years before the publication of *On the Origin of the Species.* Like his peers and contemporaries, Linnaeus believed species to be immutable.

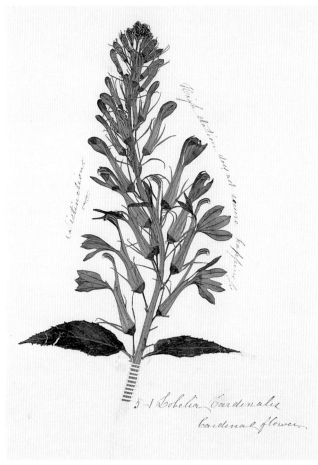

Victorian-era botanical specimens with aphorisms. left: *Asclepias incornata.* Milkweed. Inscribed "Cure for the Heartache." right: *Lobelia cardinalas.* Cardinal flower. Inscribed "Distinction—High station does not secure happiness." Each: 10 x 8 in.

From the point of view of art-collecting, a specimen or herbarium is evaluated as if it were a print, drawing, or painting: by the quality of the image(s) and by the condition of the paper—whether it is clean or soiled, damaged or pristine. In the case of a specimen, the condition of the plant itself and the quality (arrangement and neatness) of the mounting also figure in.

Documentation is desirable, particularly a date, but authorship, though potentially interesting, is rarely a factor, simply because specimens are usually unsigned. However, if one could identify a signature as belonging to, say, a noted botanist (assuming one knows something of botanical history), this would certainly add value. Inscriptions and captions giving information on collecting locations and plant descriptions also add to desirability. Sometimes an inscription has poetic value, as in the case of the specimen (shown above) of a common milkweed labeled "Cure for the Heartache." Would that it were so.

Specimens prepared by professional botanists (pages 48–59) carry extensive documentation that includes the common and botanical name, date and place collected, name of collector, and a file number, analogous to a library call number. They are also botanically complete with all parts of the plant, including root and seeds. This rigorous assemblage of plant and data evokes the whole history of botanical science whose task of taxonomy—the classifying, and naming of plants—drove hunters to the ends of the known earth.

The Plant Hunters

The early plant collectors were usually in the employ of wealthy individuals or botanical institutions, or were working for commercial nurseries. From the sixteenth to nineteenth centuries, they traversed oceans and continents in search of new and exotic plants, which they attempted—against all odds and often quite successfully—to bring home to their patrons' gardens for cultivation. They also collected specimens for scientific study and cataloging.

The majority of plant hunters were from England and Western Europe. They journeyed to Russia, North and South America, the Middle East and the Far East, at a time when sea travel was slow and hazardous, and overland travel often required pack horses or mules, porters, and canoes, and was equally fraught with discomfort and peril. Trained as either gardeners, a prominent estate position, or botanists, the plant men equipped themselves with necessary collecting paraphernalia: carrying cases for plants, cutting implements, magnifying glass, portable plant presses, drying papers, trowels and grapnels for aquatic plants and roots, sturdy gloves to protect from brambles, paper labels for specimens, and of course notebooks and maps, handbooks for identification of flora, perhaps canteens, and food containers. Taxidermy equipment might also be included, as botanists were often asked to bring home examples of local wild life as well as plants.

The first task of the scientific plant hunter was to collect specimens, essential for keeping an accurate record of the various species. These had to be expertly dried in the field and then often sent home to a specialist for mounting. (Some institutional collections today have three-hundred-year-old specimens that are in excellent condition.) Plant hunters also sent living specimens home as well, the transportation of which was another problem entirely. Sent by sea, plants could be mishandled, deprived of fresh water and sunlight, eaten by rats, and harmed by salt water. Amazingly, thousands survived to be cultivated in botanical gardens throughout Europe. But in 1834, with the invention of the Wardian case, it became feasible to ship living plants and seeds efficiently and safely over long distances.

The invention—what today is called a terrarium—was so important to botanical science and

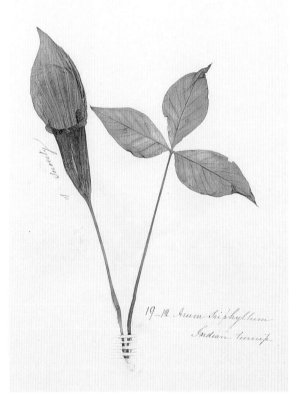

Indian turnip, nineteenth century. Inscribed "Ferocity." 10 x 8 in.

FRENCH BRONZED FLOWER STANDS, FERNERIES, WINDOW BRACKETS, &c.

1. Four cup Table Stand, $2.25.
2. Ivy Stand, 6 inch, 75 cts.; 7 inch, 85 cts.
3. Globe Stand, 5 cups, $4.00; 7 cups, $5.00.
4. Bronzed Fernery Base, (without glass,) 9 inch, $2.00; 12 inch, $3.00.
5. Flower Stand, 13 cups, $8.00.
6. Table Flower Stand, $1.50.
7. Fernery and Table, $32.00; without Table, $20.00.
8. Bronzed Ivy Bracket, 5 or 6 inch cup, 50 cts.
9. French Bronzed Flower Bracket, one cup 5 or 6 inch diameter, 75 cts.
10. French Bronzed Flower Bracket, two cups 5 or 6 inch diameter, $1.00.
11. French Bronzed Flower Bracket, three cups 5 or 6 inch diameter, $1.25.
12. French Bronzed Flower Bracket, four cups 5 or 6 inch diameter, $1.50.
13. Bird Cage Hook, 25 cts.
14. French Bronzed Aquarium, capacity 12½ gals., $16.00; with table like No. 7, $28.00.
15. Fern Case, size 17 x 14 x 13 inches, $12.50.
16. Hanging Fernery, wood with zinc pans, $6.00 $9.00 and $12.00.

Illustrated Catalogue of the above with many other beautiful designs, 36 pages—mailed to applicants enclosing 3 cent stamp.

pteridomania: fern madness
and the wardian case

Nathaniel Ward's amazing case—today known as a terrarium—became a tremendously popular commercial success in England, where it often appeared as a parlor adornment. This encouraged, some think, a curious craze for ferns, called *Pteridomania* (after the botanical name for the genus). It's easy to understand the Victorian enthusiasm for and enchantment with ferns, as they are among the most beautiful of plants. Ferns grow, romantically enough, in cool, shady glades—the quintessential fairytale setting—and are found in a multitude of forms and sizes. To house ferns in the most picturesque manner imaginable, Wardian cases were produced as dollhousesized architectural structures, some reproductions of famous buildings like Tintern Abbey and the Crystal Palace. Inevitably, this particular craze died (giving way to another—aquaria), but ferns remained one of botany's

major fields of study. In 1854, *Ferns of Great Britain and Ireland* was published with nature-printed illustrations by Henry Bradbury (see pages 110–111). It remains one of the great printing experiments of all time, highly valued for the beauty of its plates. That it was published at the height of *Pteridomania* had little to do with the craze, and everything to do with the suitability of ferns for making an impression on the printed page.

36   THE J. L. MOTT IRON WORKS, NEW YORK

CAST IRON CHAIR

Plate 50-D

FERN CHAIR

Price, with wood or iron seat.   Bronzed, $15 50   Galvanized, $18 00

The Victorian passion for ferns, and decorative Wardian cases in which to display them, is reflected, opposite, in a page from the B. K. Bliss & Sons 1876 seed catalog, which offered several styles of "ferneries." right: A cast-iron "Fern Chair" was offered by the J. L. Mott Iron Works of New York. Ephemera collection of Linda Campbell Franklin.

An eighteenth-century botanical specimen of *Banksia dentata*, an Australian evergreen collected by the legendary English botanist Sir Joseph Banks on Captain Cook's first voyage, lies on top of Banks's herbarium. Banks's cabinet, with its folders of rare pressed plants, formed the nucleus of what became England's Natural History Museum. Photo by Cary Wolinsky.

horticulture that the study of plants is now commonly divided into pre-Wardian and post-Wardian periods. Credit the Wardian case, among other prodigious accomplishments, with enabling the establishment of the East India Company's tea crop in India, for it allowed seeds to be transported from China.

The case was invented accidentally Nathaniel Ward, an amateur naturalist who lived in the then-smoggy Whitechapel section of London. Ward buried a caterpillar cocoon in earth in a sealed glass bottle and then forgot about it. Some months later, he was amazed to see small green ferns growing in the moist soil. He had happened on a phenomenon: the respiration capability of plants within a sealed or partially ventilated environment. It was now possible to protect and maintain plants and seeds over a long period of time without the need for attention.

The Wardian case greatly increased the survival rate, and therefore the quantity of plants shipped home by the plant hunters. One nineteenth-century researcher determined that of 13,140 plants cultivated in Britain, only 1,400 were native. From where, then, was this great global garden harvested? From the New World, to be sure, but also from the exotic and far-flung regions of Asia, South America, the West Indies, and beyond.

Searching the World for Plants

Botanizing in the post-classical world went through three major stages, the first of which began in the sixteenth century. An interest in finding increased sources for curative and other useful plants was fol-lowed by a concern for supplying the great gardens of Europe with ever more exotic and beautiful growths. Finally, the eighteenth century saw the full-blown age of scientific botanizing in which men—and eventually some women—traveled to the farthest reaches of the earth to find, identify, and bring back new species of plants to be studied, recorded, and written about.

The sixteenth-century French physician Pierre Belon, one of the earliest botanizers, personified the first phase of botanical exploration through his interest in medicinal plants. The garden he supervised in Le Mans contained many foreign trees and shrubs, including cedar of Lebanon and the first tobacco plants ever seen in France. In a three-year tour, Belon "established a pattern which was followed by scientific travelers for nearly three centuries" (Coats 1970, 12) by using scientific methods in his observations and records, the basis for all systematic research. But he was also concerned with inspecting exotic "curiosités," which he made note of in his subsequent writings.

In 1546, he set off on a tour of the Greek islands, Turkey, and the Middle East to study firsthand the plants and animals found in ancient Greek and Roman references. He probably did not bring back samples of seed and plants purely for scientific study, nor did he dry and mount specimens (the concept of the herbarium was still a short way in the future). But he may have been the first to introduce the tulip into European gardening circles (Pavord 1999, 58). Belon wrote descriptions and made drawings of plant samples each day, noting where he had found them and including observations about growth habits and distinctive

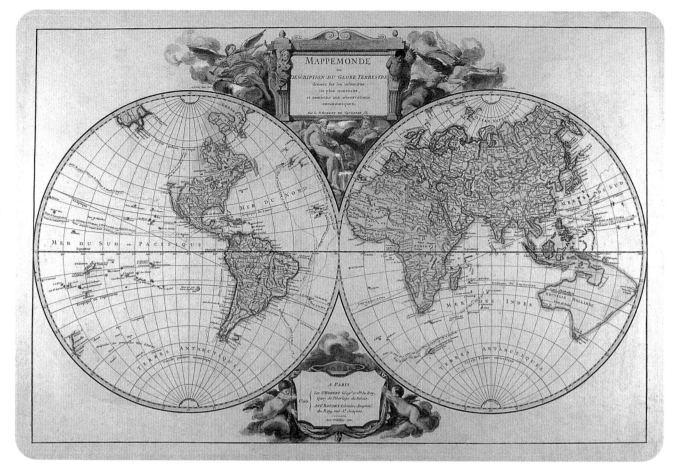

An antique double-globe map of the Americas and the Far East displays regions favored by plant hunters, who searched the world for rare and exotic flora from the sixteenth to the nineteenth centuries. Eighteenth-century French engraving. Courtesy of Swann Galleries.

characteristics. These and other commentaries were published in 1554 in the book, *Les Observations des Plusieurs Singularités* (Observations of Many Unusual Things).

But even before Belon made his trip to the Mediterrean and the Middle East, botanical explorers had begun to arrive in the New World. They were looking for the species described by classical authors, which they believed to be fixed in number and description. Clearly, the new explorers were in for an overwhelming surprise.

The flora of the New World (as well as the fauna) faced these investigators with a factual upset of vast proportions. How were they to account for the fact that familiar shrubs and trees proved on inspection to differ from known plants when their invari-

ability had been taken as an article of faith for many centuries? Perhaps even more profoundly disturbing must have been the undeniable visual proof that plants of a kind never before known stood before them, luxuriantly flourishing in the mysterious wilderness of the Western hemisphere.

In 1514, Gonzalo Fernandez de Oviedo y Valdes, a very early naturalist-explorer, investigated parts of Central America and the Caribbean for about a decade. He published the first work on his findings in 1526: *Natural History of the West Indies*, issued in English in 1555. Reflecting on the botanical concerns of the time, Oviedo wrote about plants with medicinal possibilities as well as those that were used for food by the aboriginal inhabitants. His work attracted the

attention of Sir Walter Raleigh and may well have started wheels turning in his mind.

While interest in medicinal plants continued, the following century was primarily the botanical age of discovering ever more varied and wonderful plants to furnish elaborate gardens. Scientific inquiry served as an additional focus for those who supervised and designed them; but primarily, this was the age of the great gardeners. One of the most notable among them was John Tradescant, along with his son, also named John. It was they who "set the pace." (Whittle, 29).

The elder Tradescant, born in the 1570s, was a prodigiously talented gardener. Among his aristocratic and ultimately royal employers was the earl of Salisbury, who succeeded his father, William Cecil (Baron Burghley), as the primary adviser to Queen Elizabeth I. Later, there was the duke of Buckingham, a favorite at the Jacobean court, and finally, King Charles I. The elder Tradescant may also have been one of the earliest experimenters with hybridization.

Tradescant went on a number of horticultural buying trips to France, the Netherlands, and Belgium, bringing back new species across the English Channel. But he also did some botanizing when the occasion presented itself, traveling to Russia, as well as the Greek islands, North Africa, and possibly Turkey. Among the numbers of specimens he is especially

left, top and bottom: Watercolor paintings of unidentified locales include a probable Asian landscape of palms and giant water lilies and an aquatic seascape of flourishing marine plants, sea creatures, and human remains. From a group of paintings intended as illustrations for an unpublished book, *Plant Scenery of the World: A Popular Introduction to Botanical Geography* by John Hutton Balfour and Robert Kaye Greville. 10 x 6¾ in. Collection of Post Road Gallery.

associated with are the Algiers apricot, a dramatic gladiolus species (*Gladiolus byzantinus*), and probably a variety of larch. The younger Tradescant made three trips to Virginia (in 1637, 1642, and 1654), and may have brought back as many as ninety new plants, among them the scarlet runner bean, Michaelmas daisies, and the evening primrose.

Plant explorations in America during the seventeenth century were specially marked by collecting on the part of the English. They were delighted with the botanical riches and exotica of their colonies, which offered novel and opulent species destined to fill the great gardens at home. But toward the end of the century, interest in American plants began to wane; much from North America had already been taken and planted. "Trees from Canada and New England had been in European gardens since the mid-1500s; Tradescant had brought many of the Virginian species into cultivation in the 1640s....The fickleness of the English gardener had shifted from the trees and shrubs of the New World to those of China....For a while, it was botanically quiet" (Reveal 1992, 30).

What was waiting in the wings, however, was the next wave in the New World: botanical hunting and gathering not for decoration and status trumpeting, but as an aspect of science.

above and opposite: Specimens of mosses collected with earth intact, from an 1867 herbarium of plants of the Pyrenees. above: *Funaria hygrometrica.*

Collecting in the Name of Science

With the coming of the eighteenth century, "plants were primarily collected in a spirit of scientific inquiry...The botanist's daybook and herbarium, his microscope and vascula became more important than the apothecary's laboratory and garden bed" (Whittle, 45).

In 1712, English botanist Mark Catesby traveled to the colonies to botanize and, as the first full-time professional collector, became the person most responsible for sending new American species back to England. A talent that added to his success as a naturalist was his ability to paint and draw. When he returned to England in 1726, after fourteen years spent botanizing the American southeast and parts of the Caribbean, he published his *Natural History of Carolina, Florida and the Bahama Islands*, complete with his own engravings. Interest in the book and the plants themselves was so great that it brought a London visit by Linnaeus and Catesby was honored for his accomplishments by election to the Royal Society in 1733.

The colonies at this point had not yet produced a home-grown botanizer of note. From the time of the first settlements in the early seventeenth century, the colonists were preoccupied with clearing and farming the land, fighting wars, defending themselves against sometimes hostile Indians, establishing trade and domestic commerce, and pushing westward. The absence of an American botanist on the American scene was about to be changed, however, by a man who was born just as the eighteenth century was about to dawn.

John Bartram, a Pennsylvania Quaker born in 1699, supplied Linnaeus with specimens longer than any other plant hunter. From 1735 to 1778, he sent the great Swedish naturalist box after box of consistently "new and exciting plants" (Reveal, 49).

But Linnaeus was hardly the only beneficiary of his talents. Bartram supplied many if not most of the aristocratic gardens in England through his arrangements with Peter Collinson, a London textile dealer and horticultural enthusiast who had a wide network of collectors and prodigious correspondence. It was Collinson who had underwritten the publication of Mark Catesby's work, and it was Collinson who gave Bartram his start.

Bartram set aside five acres for a botanical garden on his farm on the Schuykill River a few miles from Philadelphia. He called it his "garden of delight" and it was initially dominated by medicinal plants. Bartram was both self-taught as well as educated by others, and the more he learned, the more he began to search for plants that he could cultivate himself. When Collinson was searching for American sources, Bartram

Entosthodon fascicularis Dicks.
1ᵉ Béat- Printemps.

was brought to his attention. Collinson supplied Bartram with field equipment, tools, books, and—most of all—sound advice that Bartram took to heart. He became an astute collector, and increasingly grew to understand the scientific aspects of what he foraged.

Bartram experimented successfully with hybridization, starting in the 1730s. He also honed his gathering techniques to improve the quality of seeds he sent abroad. The samples he sent were often of superb quality.

A simple, yet canny, country man, John Bartram became one of the major botanists of the eighteenth century. He managed to balance the demands of his farm with the call of collecting, botanizing through Virginia, the Carolinas, Georgia, Florida, Pennsylvania, New Jersey, and New York, accompanied eventually by his son William who was eager to become a botanist and who showed signs of ability in the field. One of the elder Bartram's fondest wishes was to be appointed the king's botanist; a desire that was finally realized in 1765, twelve years before he died.

America's next great botanizer came to the newly United States of America from France. André Michaux, son of an estate manager at Versailles, turned to botany and travel in 1770, in an effort to bury his grief over the death of his young wife. One of

Muhlenbergia microsperma (DC) Kunth

DETERMINED BY CHARLOTTE G. REEDER   Dec. 1972

TERRITORIO SUR de BAJA CALIFORNIA
MEXICO
Muhlenbergia adpressa
C. O. Goodding

Cape Region. La Laguna. Large meadow
surrounded by a forest of oaks and
Pinus cembroides. Alt. about 6000 feet.
Dry parts of meadow.

110°
0 10 20 mi.

La Paz
24°
San Pedro
San Bartolo
La Laguna
Todos   Santi-
Santos   ago
Caduaño
N
Santa
Anita
San José
del Cabo
23°
San Lucas

7921 John H. Thomas   May 16-18, 1959

his mentors was Louis-Guillaume le Monnier, physician to the King of France and director of the Jardin du Roi. After plans for a trip to Mexico failed, Michaux traveled to the Middle East. En route overland from Aleppo, Syria, in 1785, he managed to forage despite adverse conditions, and arrived in Baghdad later that year with seeds of one hundred species of desert plants. When he arrived back in France, he was received at the French court, accorded honors, and given an honorarium. But Michaux was not a man to rest on his botanical samples; he was off to the United States two months later.

Headquartering in Charleston, South Carolina, he botanized the length of eastern North America, from Florida in the south to Hudson's Bay in the Canadian north. He foraged in Kentucky, crossed the Tennessee wilderness, and eventually arrived at the Mississippi River, which stood as the great dividing line between plant hunting in the East, and botanical explorations of the West.

above: A variety of fern fronds. Birmingham, England, nineteenth century. 13 x 12 in.

opposite: Botanical specimen. Mexican grasses mounted with a hand-drawn map that pinpoints locations collected.

By the summer of 1796, ruined by the French Revolution and without funds to sustain him in America, Michaux set out for France. Caught in a storm, he survived his ship's wreck by being lashed to a mast; miraculously, a large consignment of plants and specimens was saved as well. At home again, he wrote *Histoire des Chenes d'Amerique* (Oaks of America), published in 1801, and completed *Flora Boreali Americana* (North American Flora) two years later, shortly before he died of a fever while botanizing in Madagascar.

Although Michaux's flora of the United States, posthumously published in 1803, was the first extensive work on the subject, it quickly became outdated as exploration of the continent increased. *Genera of North American Plants* by Thomas Nuttall, published in 1818, enlarged and improved on Michaux's work.

Nuttall was a printer from Liverpool, England, who emigrated to Philadelphia—then the publishing capital of the New World—in 1808, when he was twenty-two years old. Soon after his arrival, an interest in botany surfaced, and he began study with the eminent Philadelphia naturalist, Benjamin Smith Barton. It was Barton who had been tutor to

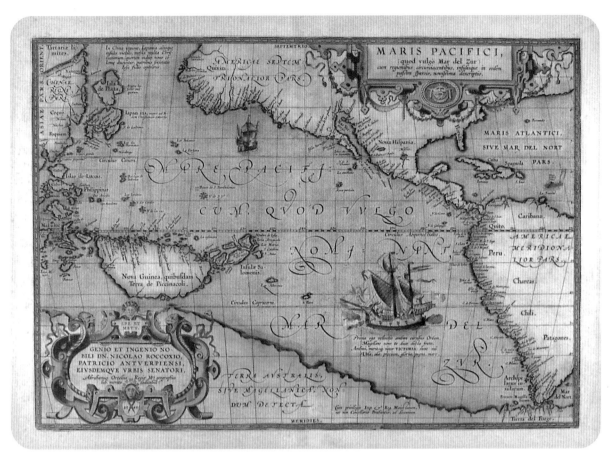

An antique map of the Pacific, complete with Magellan's ship, *Victoria*, encompasses regions popular with nineteenth-century botanical explorers. Sixteenth-century hand-colored engraving. Courtesy of Swann Galleries.

Meriwether Lewis, preparing him for the botanical aspects of the great westward expedition Lewis led with William Clark.

By 1809, Nuttall had started botanizing and contracted to send Barton his specimens, seeds, and notes. His eagerness to become a botanical explorer and his physical courage and success on wide-ranging and sometimes dangerous trips is all the more impressive in light of the fact that Nuttall had no idea what to expect on the frontier, did not know how to shoot, could not swim, and possibly never learned.

Nuttall's work represents a critical point in North American botanical exploration. He was one of the first, if not the very first major botanist to cross over the seemingly fixed dividing line that separated East and West to explore plants across the breadth,

and much of the length, of the continental United States and the frontier.

Realizing that the botanical books he had been reading were out of date, he wrote his *Genera of North American Plants*, setting most of the type himself. In the early 1820s, Nuttall was appointed to a professorship in natural history at Harvard University and also became curator of Harvard's botanical garden. Chafing, one suspects, at the confinement of academic and town life, he nonetheless wrote a textbook, *An Introduction to Systematic and Physiological Botany*, and—as he had become an expert on birds during his botanical explorations—completed most of his *Manual of the Ornithology of the United States and Canada* during his tenure.

But when the opportunity arose for another exploration, this time to Oregon in 1834, Nuttall took a leave of absence. After two years, the trip, which extended through much of the Far West, with winters spent in Hawaii, must have struck the college as an overly long sabbatical; it was requested· that Nuttall resign his professorship. The position was eventually filled in 1842 by Asa Gray, who became director of the now-famous herbarium at Harvard that bears his name.

In 1841, Nuttall inherited the estate of an uncle in England. His financial situation was too precarious to refuse the bequest, which stipulated that he had to spend nine months of every year on the property. Nuttall was a passionate and obsessive botanist; to no longer practice the occupation that had shaped his life and brought him his greatest joys must have seemed like a cruel irony. Still, he made the best use he could of his annual three free months and tended the garden where he cultivated his favorite American plants until his death in 1859.

David Douglas: The Adventures of the Grass Man

Thomas Nuttall was by no means the first to botanize in the western United States. One of his predecessors was David Douglas,[8] considered by many to be one of the greatest plant collectors who ever lived. He is honored because of the magnitude and thoroughness of his collecting, which he accomplished virtually unaided and despite great personal hardship. Douglas's most noteworthy collecting was done in the 1820s in the Pacific Northwest. He traveled alone most of the time, relying exclusively on native wit, toughness, and his own finely tuned powers of botanical observation. It is estimated that he traveled roughly twelve thousand miles, mostly on foot with only a pack horse or two to carry his specimens. Dozens of plant and tree species are named for him, most notably the Douglas fir, which is just one of many pines he discovered along the Pacific coast. He is credited with discovering a third of the great western conifers,

In a collotype from a book, seemingly minuscule human figures dramatize the immense size of the Douglas fir, named for the intrepid Scottish botanist David Douglas.

---

[8]A detailed and entertaining account of Douglas's life and adventures is contained in William Morewood's *Traveler in a Vanished Landscape: The Life & Times of David Douglas, Botanical Explorer.* Morewood's close reading of Douglas's journals set against historical records has led him to interpolate and question many accepted aspects of Douglas's own stories and the legends that surround him. This section draws largely from that book.

The New York Botanical Garden
INSTITUTE OF ECONOMIC BOTANY
Merck Collections and Extractions

STRELITZIACEAE

Ravenala madagascariensis Sonn.
    det. Daniel Atha. 1996

BELIZE. Cayo District. Near Ix Chel Farm. ca. 8km south of
San Ignacio on bank of Macal river. 17°06'N. 89°04'W.
200m. Growing amongst other ornamentals. Cultivated.

Herb to 6m. large: leaves 1-ranked: flowers and fruits
arising from leaf axils.

n.v.: None reported.
USE: None reported.
Merck Sample codes: 212a LF(Meleady-43): 212b petiole(Meleady-44)
212c FR(Meleady-45): 212d peduncle(Meleady-46)

Peter E. Meleady 212   May 31. 1996
with Daniel Atha. Javier Cordero

Fieldwork supported by Merck and Co., Inc. Voucher for pharmaceutical
screening.

including the western larch, ponderosa pine, noble fir, and sugar pine, and introduced over two hundred species into modern horticulture. There is hardly a category of plants, from Alaska to the Mexican border, that does not have a species named for Douglas, either in his honor or because he discovered it (Morewood 1973, 40).

The story of David Douglas embodies all of the passion and persistence needed to endure the rigors of plant hunting. Born to a poor family in Scone, Scotland, in 1798, Douglas's tenacity and stubbornness had been evident from early childhood. The son of a stone mason, he so misbehaved that his mother sent him to school at the age of three, just to have him out of the house. A practiced truant at ten, he quit school permanently and found a job as an apprentice to the head gardener at the Palace of Scone. There Douglas swiftly developed a passion for natural history and an aptitude for gardening, along with an improved temperament, and within seven years he had determined to become a botanist. Douglas so impressed William Hooker, then a professor of botany at the Glasgow Botanical Garden and the eventual director of Kew Gardens, that he recommended him for a position at the new Horticultural Society of London.

opposite and pages 51, 52, and 55: A selection of specimens from the herbarium of the New York Botanical Garden demonstrate not only the beauty of natural forms, but also professional techniques for mounting oversized and thick-stemmed plants, complete with paper seed packets, and proper identification. Shown here is botanical specimen *Ravenia madagascariensis.* Collected May 31, 1996. New York Botanical Garden.

In 1823, the society's director sent Douglas to find and collect fruit trees and flowering annuals of the eastern United States that would be suitable for cultivation in the "natural" landscapes of English gardens. Douglas more than proved his mettle on this first trip, returning with no less than twenty-one varieties of peaches and ten varieties of apples, plus assorted cuttings and seeds. He was rewarded with an almost immediate dispatch to the Pacific Northwest, where he spent four adventurous years of botanical discovery; years fraught with natural disasters, loneliness, narrow escapes, and severe personal injury. A journal entry from that period reads: "...travelled thirty-three miles drenched and bleached with rain and sleet, chilled with a piercing north wind; and then to finish the day experienced the cool comfortless consolation of lying down wet without supper or fire. On such occasions I am very liable to become fretful."

In search of plants, Douglas forded icy rivers, crossed the Rockies in snow shoes, endured blistering heat in southern California, suffered arthritis and progressive near-blindness, survived the overturning of his canoe—and the loss of his precious botanical notes and "observances" in the treacherous rapids of the Fraser River—all of which damaged his body but never entirely his spirit.

For most of the decade between 1824 and 1834, Douglas traveled the West and sent numerous important finds back to England. He is especially known for extraordinary diligence in searching out every possible species of a single plant. He collected eighteen species of Penstemmons, and discovered the wild peony (*paeonia bronii*) as well as the flowering currant, one of the most important annuals ever introduced into cultivation in England.

"Feeling great-broken" as he wrote in his diary after the loss of his research in the Fraser River, he sailed for the Sandwich Islands (Hawaii) where he knew he would eventually have to get a boat home to England. But fate dealt him a different hand.

In July 1834, Douglas awaited a ship bound for England. On a climb of Mauna Kea, he encountered Edward Gurney, an ex-convict who lived in a hut on the mountain, who warned Douglas about the danger of cattle pits in the area. Deep and camouflaged, they were used to entrap wild bulls that roamed the island. Douglas set off with his dog Billy, who had accompanied him on many trips, and was never seen alive again. Searchers found his bloodied body at the bottom of a pit , trampled by an enraged bull. Billy sat nearby, guarding Douglas's pack.

Despite his tragic death, Douglas's name lives in the hundreds of plants and trees he collected, and in the annals of collecting where he is considered one of the greatest and most productive adventurers. The specimens he expertly preserved may be viewed in museums today.

The Pacific and Beyond

In stark contrast to Douglas and the many other plant hunters who lived by their wits alone, was the dashing Sir Joseph Banks, who made botanical explorations of the South Pacific, Tahiti, New Zealand, and Australia with Captain Cook from 1768 to 1771. Banks laid the groundwork for establishing England as the "center of horticultural discovery" (Healey 1975, 65) in the nineteenth century, and "enlarged the Western world's knowledge of existing plant species by nearly twenty-five percent" (Watkins 1996, 36). He also encouraged the movement of plants among nations in what is termed antipodean exchange. The most famous example of this occurred on the 1787 voyage of the HMS *Bounty* to the South Pacific under Captain William Bligh, where he was charged with gathering breadfruit to be replanted in the British West Indies as food for slaves (Watkins, 50).

A true mover and shaker in his time, Banks used his considerable influence and fortune to direct, both formally and informally, several of England's scientific and botanical institutions. He was the longest-serving president of the Royal Society in London, and, with the support of George III, made the Royal Botanic Garden at Kew one of the world's foremost herbariums and collections of living plants. Under Banks's honorary directorship of Kew, collectors were trained, and the number of species in cultivation exceeded 10,000. He established the commonwealth of Australia, and a shrub native to New Zealand, *banksia,* is named for him.

One of Banks's special contributions to botanical art and science was the florilegium that resulted from his tour aboard the HMS *Endeavour* with Captain Cook. Banks had the forsight to bring two artists, Sydney Parkinson and Alexander Buchan (in addition to a secretary and four assistant collectors), to draw

opposite: Botanical specimen. *Nelumbo lutca.* Lotus seed pods. New York Botanical Garden.

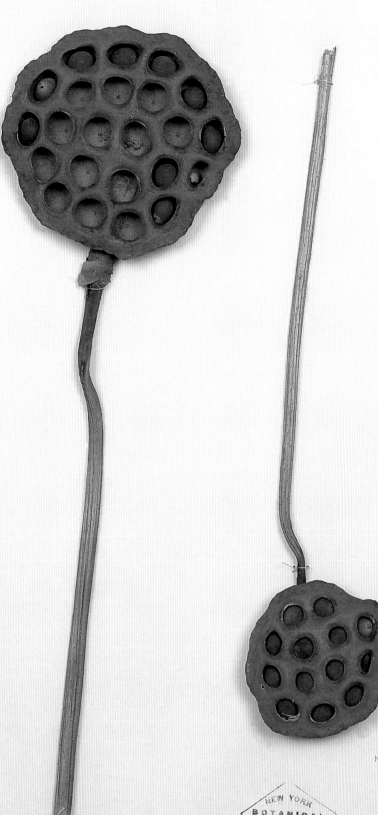

NELUMBO LUTCA / WILLD / PERS.

NO: 753

ROBERT A. EVERS

10611
40
II

THE NEW YORK BOTANICAL GARDEN GUIANA EXPLORATIONS
PLANTS OF BRITISH GUIANA
UPPER MAZARUNI RIVER BASIN

No. 44894

Nymphaea ampla (Salisb.) DC.

Older leaves floating, leaves green to olive green
above, reddish beneath, bud only, petals apparently
white above pink beneath. Only 3 seen.
Harika savanna in small clear water stream East of
Harika River.

Ayanganna Plateau.

Stephen S. Tillett   July 21, 1980
Carolyn L. Tillett

Field work conducted with the cooperation of the Departments of Forestry and Interior, British Guiana.
Supported in part by funds provided by the National Science Foundation.

examples of island flora in situ. Although 743 engraved plates were completed from the drawings in Banks's lifetime, it was only in 1988 that the complete *Banks Florilegium* was published, in full-color, under the aegis of the Natural History Museum in London (Watkins, 49). Banks was the patron of a number of other artists, among them Franz Bauer, who in 1790 became, at Banks's expense, the official draftsman of Kew. Bauer's drawings became part of Banks's bequest, which, together with his herbarium and library, became the nucleus of the botanical department of the museum.

After Banks died in 1820, Kew fell into decline until it was taken in hand by its first official director, Sir William Hooker, in 1841. Hooker's appointment was in effect a posthumous triumph for Banks, who, twenty years earlier, had obtained for him a professorship in botany at the Glasgow Botanical Garden.

Sir William Hooker, together with his son Joseph Dalton Hooker, did much to establish Kew as the world's leading botanical institution in the nineteenth century. Sir William is credited with three major achievements: establishing Kew as a public museum with informative guides to the gardens; creating an unsurpassed herbarium and library; and transforming Kew into a "horticultural mecca" (Desmond 1995, 222). Like Banks, he encouraged the transfer of plants, specifically that of cinchona, a source of quinine, from South America to India. He enlarged Kew's vast and varied collections of living plants by sending collectors, including his son, to key areas that included Jamaica and Colombia, Japan and China, and India.

Joseph Dalton Hooker had, by the age of twenty-two, botanized in the Antarctic on an exploration that, from 1839 to 1843, had pinpointed the location of the south magnetic pole. A skilled scientist, he assisted Charles Darwin's research, and in 1848 made a notable collecting trip to India, sending back important specimens of orchids and forty-three species of rhododendrons. His book, *Rhododendrons of the Sikkim Himalaya* revealed for the first time the beauty of a plant that would captivate western gardeners. He also undertook the formidable task of mapping the eastern Himalayas, wrote the *Flora of British India* (1897), and published a handbook to the flora of Ceylon. Joseph succeeded his father as director of Kew in 1865, and held the position for twenty years, although he was a reluctant administrator, preferring the active pursuits of science above all else.

The Lure of Asia   While North America yielded untold botanical treasures for English and European gardens, the ultimate trophy plants lay in the Orient—primarily China and Japan, but also India. Flowers pictured on Chinese and Japanese ceramics and textiles had long intrigued plant hunters, who were eager to acquire examples of lush roses and peonies, exquisite camillias, and varieties of flowering trees. Forays by British and Europeans into the tightly controlled regions of Asia began in the seventeenth century, but it was not until the nineteenth century that plant collectors had their greatest collecting success.

opposite: Botanical specimen. *Nymphae ampla.* July 21, 1960. New York Botanical Garden.

One of the most productive collectors in Asia was Robert Fortune, a Scot who worked mainly for English institutions and nurseries. A professional gardener, his skills in packing and shipping plants were much in demand, and he made three trips to China for different clients between 1843 and 1858. On his first trip for the Royal Horticultural Society, where he was superintendent of the hothouses at Chiswich, he succeed in penetrating the northern provinces. There he found hills glowing with azaleas. Although inland travel was forbidden to foreigners, Fortune disguised himself some of the time as a Chinese and, over a period of three years was able to collect important examples of the moutan, or tree peony, *Camillia sinensis*, winter jasmine, bleeding heart, plums, and primulas. An effective manager, Fortune also hired Chinese men to collect for him while he himself acted as clearinghouse. He wrote of his high adventures and narrow escapes in a book, *Three Years Wandering in the Northern Provinces of China*, which was published in 1847. In that same year he became curator of the Chelsea Physic Garden, but in 1848, he was asked by the British East India Company to return to China to collect tea plants and seeds. Fortune was able to send two thousand plants and seventeen thousand seedlings, packed in Wardian cases, to Calcutta, where they became the basis of the British tea industry in India. He began one more trip in 1858 for the American government, which also sought tea plants for cultivation, but the impending Civil War aborted his trip.

In 1860, Fortune was one of many botanists to travel to Japan, which in 1853 had opened its door to foreigners for the first time in two hundred years. Fortune traveled from the port of Nagasaki to Yokohama and finally to Tokyo, where he visited nurseries and made purchases of chrysanthemums. From there he returned to England, but revisited Japan in the spring for the British nursery Standish & Noble of Bagshot. He was captivated by the profusion of flowering plants, writing "Never at any one time had I met with so many really fine plants" (Coats, 74). Among the floral treasures that Fortune obtained was the *Lilium auratum* (golden-rayed lily), which he found on the way to Kamakura.

During his travels in Japan, Fortune encountered John Gould Veitch, the great-grandson of the famed Veitch family who owned nurseries in Chelsea. Like other collectors, Veitch found himself unable to travel freely, but despite imposed limitations assembled a magnificent collection of twenty-five species of conifers, including both seeds and specimens. He, like many other collectors, was smitten with the golden-ray lily, which became one of the firm's great successes. When John Gould died at an early age, the Veitch dynasty was carried on by his eldest son, James Harry Veitch, who in 1891–1892 made a world tour that brought him to Japan. He was astounded at the extent of the Tokyo nurseries, which he noted were larger than those in Flanders or in Holland. By that time, the Japanese had fully understood the commercial value of their plants and had established a thriving export trade in bulbs.

opposite: Botanical specimen. *Passiflora aff. Biflora.* Collected November 12, 1977. New York Botanical Garden.

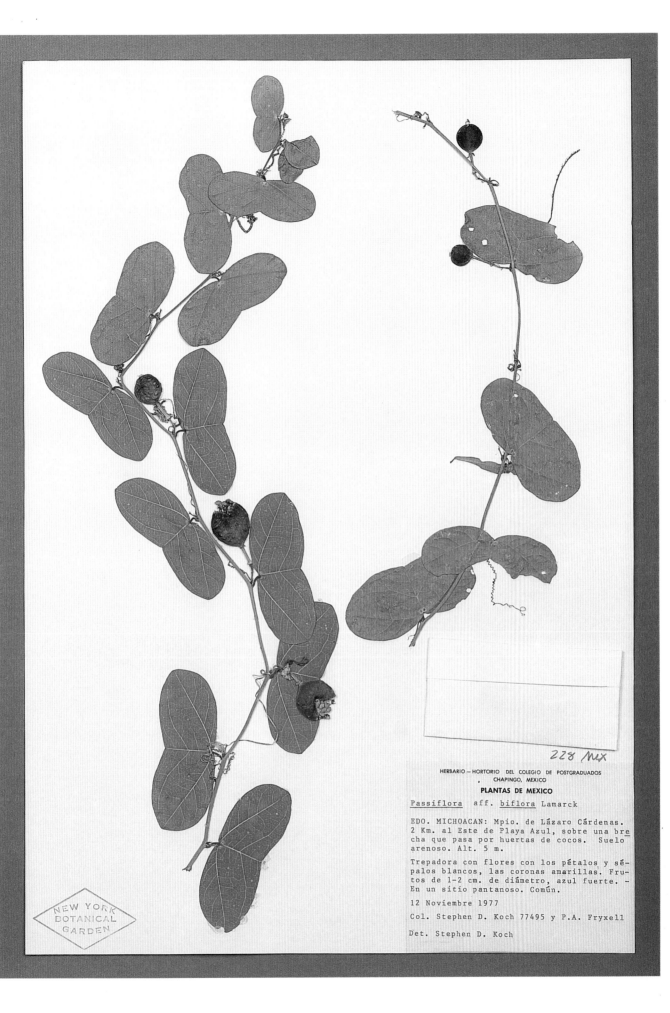

228 Mex

<u>Passiflora</u> aff. <u>biflora</u> Lamarck

EDO. MICHOACAN: Mpio. de Lázaro Cárdenas.
2 Km. al Este de Playa Azul, sobre una bre
cha que pasa por huertas de cocos. Suelo
arenoso. Alt. 5 m.

Trepadora con flores con los pétalos y sé-
palos blancos, las coronas amarillas. Fru-
tos de 1-2 cm. de diámetro, azul fuerte. -
En un sitio pantanoso. Común.

12 Noviembre 1977

Col. Stephen D. Koch 77495 y P.A. Fryxell

Det. Stephen D. Koch

A. F. Jones.

Historically, the Chinese had granted Roman-Catholic missionaries special privileges as foreign residents, but until 1860, they had been denied access to western mountain provinces (Whittle, 206). The first to be granted permission to explore and proselytize in these wild regions was Jean Pierre Armand David, a Lazarist in the Order of St. Vincent de Paul. The archetype of the missionary-botanist, David was trained as a science teacher. His scientific talents became well known in France, so that at age thirty-five, when he was being sent to China to establish a school of science in Peking, five members of the Natural History Museum in Paris asked him to "send back anything of interest" (Healey, 103).

David arrived in Peking in 1862 and did indeed send back such interesting specimens, and in such quantity, that the museum's scientists obtained official government sponsorship to enable him to collect full-time, "for the glory of France." (Whittle, 208). David ventured first to Mongolia, traveling with only one or

two Christian Chinese to assist him in a dangerous wilderness where wolves were so prevalent his donkey had to be taken into the tent at night. Although David found the plateau a desolate place, he made an extensive study of its flora, fauna, and geology and found silkworms "genuinely wild" (Coats, 111).

His next trip to the borders of Tibet was much more successful, as he discovered flora "richer than he could possibly have foreseen" (Whittle, 209). Realizing his opportunity, David decided to collect systematically, applying scientific methods; he was the first botanist working in Asia to do so. He collected over two thousand specimens, which represented the largest herbarium sent to Europe from Asia at that time. Among the botanical treasures he found in Tibet were rhododendron in many varieties and his odd namesake tree, the *Davidia*, with blooms like white folded handkerchiefs.

Following, almost literally, in David's footsteps, although some thirty years later, was Ernest Henry Wilson, nicknamed "Chinese Wilson" because of his extensive explorations in China (Wells 1997, 124). He is called the first modern collector because, although he customarily hired a mule train and coolies, and rode in a sedan chair (considered important for prestige) during

above and opposite: Beautifully mounted specimens from an 1850 herbarium, West Newton. above: *Virginian avens;* opposite: *Alpina enchantus.* Nightshade family. 17½ x 11½.

his Asian explorations, he also packed a cumbersome full-plate camera, lugging it into the wilderness and up and down mountains in search of floral treasures.

Wilson was educated at an early age as a plant collector at botanical gardens in England and by the Veitch nurseries, which trained him in rigorous methodology. Veitch sent him on his first trip—to China—by way of the Arnold Arboretum in Boston, where he was instructed to consult with Professor Charles Sprague Sargent, who was knowledgeable about the Orient. Wilson and Sargent struck up an immediate friendship, and Wilson would eventually work as a collector for Sargent, but not until he had completed two trips for Veitch. The first, in 1899, was to find the intriguing *Davidia*—variously called the dove tree, ghost tree, and pocket handkerchief tree, for its hood-shaped flowers—that had been discovered in the late 1860s by the French missionary, Armand David. Wilson was instructed to retrace David's steps and bring back seeds for cultivation in England. He succeeded in finding at least a species of the botanical oddity, and also managed to photograph it, having hauled his camera up a rocky precipice, and into the tree with ropes, to do so. Later, while traveling on the Yang-tze-kiang River in a sampan, the boat overturned in rapids and the camera and glass negatives were lost (Whittle, 221). Wilson replaced the camera as soon as possible—he never let calamities deter him—and continued his work. Although he found himself suddenly hemmed in by the Boxer Rebellion, which sought to oust all foreigners from China, the efficient and ever resourceful botanist managed to send back seeds for the *Davidia* and hundreds of other species, plus thirty-five Wardian cases of bulbs and rootstock and over nine hundred pressed and dried botanical specimens (Whittle, 221). His stunning accomplishment earned him another Veitch assignment soon after, this time to hunt for the Chinese poppy, which he found along with primulas and roses. Wilson emigrated to America in 1909 and in 1910 made a final China trip for the Arnold Arboretum. His quarry this time was the elegantly colored regal lily, whose flower was white inside but purple-brown-colored outside. Its introduction into modern gardening, where it remains highly favored, is entirely attributable to Wilson. He found it growing wild in a high valley in Szechuan, where he dug out almost seven thousand bulbs. As he was progressing with his mule train down a narrow mountain path with this precious cargo, he suffered a broken leg in an avalanche. Unable to move out of the way of another mule train heading in the opposite direction, Wilson directed his coolies to leave him lying in the path and have the mules, forty of them, step over his body, which they did without mishap. His leg healed imperfectly, however, causing what he called his "lily limp."

Wilson traveled twice more to Japan for the Arnold Arboretum and eventually became assistant director there. Professor Sargent's account of Wilson's valuable introductions of woody plants to the arboretum, *Plantae Wilsonianae*, was published in three volumes. Wilson died in 1930 in a car accident in Worcester, Massachusetts.

opposite: Botanial specimen. *Desmonucus Brittonii.* Collected in the West Indies, November 26, 1920. New York Botanical Garden.

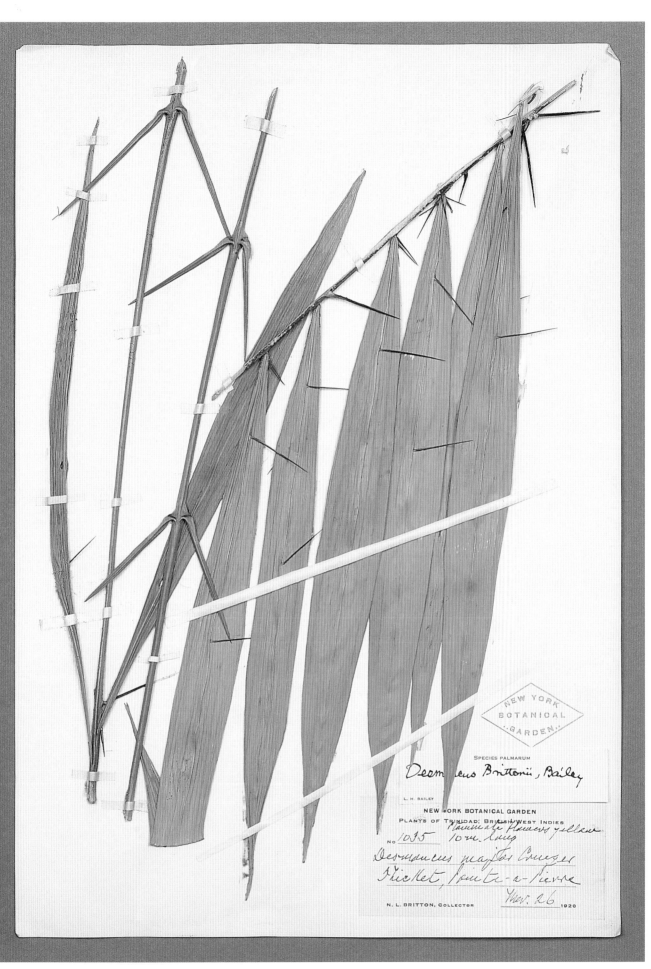

SPECIES PALMARUM

Desmoncus Brittonii, Bailey

L. H. BAILEY

NEW YORK BOTANICAL GARDEN

PLANTS OF TRINIDAD: BRITISH WEST INDIES

No. 1035   Staminate flowers yellow
10 m. long

Desmoncus major Crueger

Thicket, Pointe-a-Pierre

N. L. BRITTON, COLLECTOR   Nov. 26   1920

zen and the art of botanical specimens

The form of a pressed plant on a page can resemble the ancient Asian art technique known as *sumi,* or ink painting. *Sumi* artists use black ink, much as calligraphers do, to produce dynamic, monochromatic images, usually of plants, animals, and insects. *Sumi-e* ("ink picture") developed around the seventh century A.D. after Japanese scholars had seen it used in China. The four "strands," or strokes, of sumi are called the Four Gentlemen: Bamboo, Wild Orchid, Chrysanthemum, and Plum Branch. The Chinese believe that the Four Gentlemen stand for all known shapes and forms in the universe. And it is said the plum symbolizes the perfect gentleman: understated, free of flamboyance, and strong enough to be able to "bloom" in the face of adversity. *Sumi-e* has long been used as a Zen exercise in which the artist meditates on the form to be painted before attempting to draw it. The

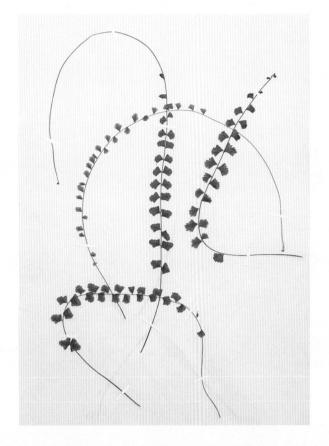

result of fine *sumi-e* is an impressionistic image in which depth and color are suggested, and spirit of the plant, or other subject, is fully expressed through the immediacy of the brushstroke. In this silk scroll painting, *Flowering Plum Branches,* by Tani Buncho, dated to a spring day in 1816, the blossoms are merely suggested and new growth springs out of the gnarled branch created from a single sweep of the brush.

above: Botanical specimen. Tendrils of a young fern have all the spontaneity of a *sumi-e* painting. From a Birmingham, England, book of ferns, nineteenth century. 12 x 13 in.

opposite: Silk scroll painting. *Flowering Plum Branches.* Tani Buncho, 1816. Exclusive of mount: 42 x 2 x 28⅛ in. Courtesy of Suzanne Mitchell Asian Fine Art.

The celebration of gardens and gardening in today's world is a tribute to these and many other plant hunters who discovered, and brought into cultivation, thousands of floral treasures.

Botanizing: The Amateurs

Starting in the early nineteenth century, ordinary people, many of them amateur botanists, found themselves caught up in the fervor of the rapidly evolving field of natural history, of which botany was a major component. A botanical sensibility was definitely in the air, one that promoted interest in gathering and mounting specimens and creating herbaria using the same methods as the renowned plant hunters. Botany was the science most accessible and comprehensible to the layman. The methodology was fairly simple, it required only minimal equipment, and it was important work that welcomed, even courted, the contributions of amateurs. Botanizing afforded an opportunity to experience the beauties of the natural world in an invigorating outdoor environment, but also a chance to improve one's mind—and perhaps soul. Botanizing's central activity was collecting plants in the wild and preserving specimens using the Linnaean system of classification. By the 1820s in America, collecting clubs had sprung up along with networks for exchange of specimens.[9] As the focus was on self-improvement, botany was embraced by the lyceum movement, which fostered adult education through lectures and symposiums sponsored by local associations of educated men and women.

The amateur botanists, who probably numbered in the thousands, were by necessity literate and somewhat financially independent, enough to be able to purchase handbooks of flora and the minimal equipment needed for collecting specimens. Their numbers included men and young people who were being taught botany through textbooks, magazines, and newspapers, but many were woman for whom the discovery of botany led to richly fulfilling lives, literally in the field, which in many cases was atypical for the nineteenth-century woman.

Women in Botany: a Life Among the Plants

"Grasses all about rejoiced my heart." Agnes Chase remarked that on a trip to Brazil. Her life, whatever its struggles, was also one long hallelujah. She had found botany.

Numbers of women in the nineteenth century found pleasure in what was a cherished pastime. For some, though, like Agnes Chase, botany was the path to a larger life, whether they started young, like Alice Eastwood, who discovered botany as a six-year-old motherless girl about to be sent off to relatives; or had reached late middle age like Ynes Mexia.[10]

---

[9] Through a meticulously documented social history, Keeney (1992) develops the thesis that American botanizing drew amateur and professional scientists together, then drove them apart with the professionalization of the field.

[10] Marcia Myers Bonta, a writer and self-taught naturalist—as many of the early women botanizers were—has written a perceptive and highly readable account of the remarkable women who made the sciences of the natural world their stage. The section on the lives of women botanists in her book (1991) was the primary source for the stories here.

In the nineteenth century in America, women found themselves with more leisure than would have been possible earlier on a farm or at the frontier. As industrial development grew in the 1800s, women in comfortably situated families were expected to acquire polite accomplishments. The desire for self-improvement propelled women toward both education and edification through school curricula and public lectures.

Botany had characteristics that helped to make it popular as a science, as well as a diversion in the nineteenth century. Botanizers found innocent pleasure and glowing cheeks in going out into nature to discover, identify, and press plants, and they filled the Sunday landscape. Some, however, went much farther than the fields and woods beyond town; some traveled to the far reaches of the earth. Among them were a handful of very unusual women.

"There was no denying that botanizing held a special appeal for women and girls, not just in relation to other scientific hobbies but in absolute terms," Elizabeth Keeney maintains (69). Not the least attraction was that "women would prove freer to botanize than to do many other things....Botany was considered the most genteel...of the sciences" (Keeney, 71).

This 1947 botanical specimen of a grass bears the stamp of the National Herbarium of Mexico. 16½ x 11½ in.

Botany was indeed a decorous pastime in the general view. Yet at a time when women were neither expected nor encouraged to exercise too sturdy an intellect, they seemed to have no trouble learning the Linnaean taxonomy for their plants.

Living specimens also furthered the art of flower painting. Yet when precise, detailed, and lifelike enough, these watercolors or ink drawings moved beyond the aims of a feminine art and became a way of documenting serious botanical texts or preserving in graphic form the flora of an area.

Kate Furbish was one of those who found her independence in botanical art. She did not wish to conduct her life exactly as the ladies of her hometown of Brunswick, Maine, expected. She began in 1870, when she was thirty-six, inspired by a series of lectures she had earlier heard in Boston. By the time she put aside her botanizing tools, she had gone a long way toward her goal of gathering and cataloging the plants of Maine. There were few corners of the state, however rugged, she had not penetrated.

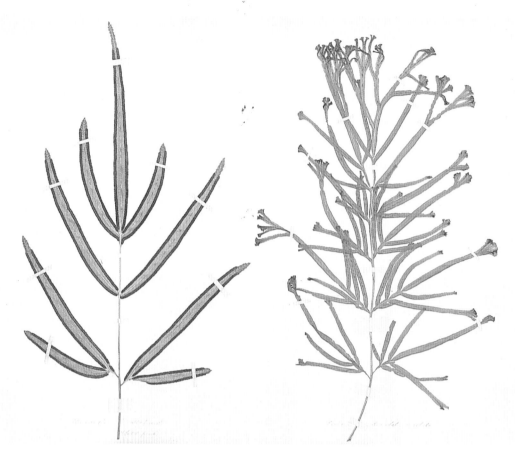

Botanical specimens. Ferns. English, nineteenth century. Approximately 8 x 10 in.

As with the women botanists who followed, the contrasts in her life were great: their time was divided between civilization and wilderness. When Kate came home and doffed her rubber boots and mud-caked clothing, she put on a ladylike dress and pressed her specimens, or sat down at an easel in a pretty, wall-papered room to paint them. Her collection of four thousand dried plants ended up at the Gray Herbarium at Harvard; her sixteen volumes of botanical watercolors went to Bowdoin College in Maine. Even after disbursing her work, she continued doing some collecting until she was ninety, reluctant to give up what had defined her life.

Quantitatively, the efforts of this small group cannot compare with the accomplishments of their male colleagues, who in vastly greater numbers foraged and discovered in every corner of the world from the late sixteenth century on. Yet these women not only made a mark botanically but culturally as well; their lives became models of possibility and achievement for women coming up.

Concomitant developments such as taking jobs as teachers or becoming active in the women's reform movement often involved "moves away form the home," and this "slowly, yet dramatically, expanded women's sphere" (Keeney, 77). Furthermore, as women "pursued botany, they expanded the range of acceptable female behavior" (82).

There were two groups of women with an interest well beyond the amateur who became involved in the field of botany in the nineteenth century. One group included botany only as part of a broader range of natu-

Botanical specimens. Ferns. English, nineteenth century. Approximately 8 x 10 in.

ral history interests. Among several of these better-known naturalists was Mary Treat, born in 1830, who supported herself thoughout an undependable marriage by writing about nature. Insects were her favorite subject, and through them she became an authority on carnivorous plants. She had a considerable correspondence with eminent scientists, among them Asa Gray, and Charles Darwin, who shared her interest in plants that ate creatures.

Another of the broad-based naturalists was Annie Montague Alexander, who was born in 1867 and grew up in Hawaii and California. A woman of great energy, she established a zoological museum for the University of California, and later, the university's museum of paleontology, keeping both well supplied. She did not turn ardently to botanical collection until

she was in her seventies, and eventually sent to the university's herbarium almost eighteen thousand specimens.

Then there was the other group—those who had a clear and single-minded calling to botany itself, botany alone. And once they discovered it, there was no looking back. The richly layered possibilities of the science called upon a variety of responses, from physical stamina and courage to a great eye and a fine intellect. It was a life that would offer a broadly balanced existence and many rewards. These were women who had fallen in love with the whole blooming world.

Another botanist called Kate, Mary Katherine Brandegee was a young widow with a medical degree that was not paying off in patients. She turned to botany, studying at the California Academy of Sciences. In 1883, when she was in her late thirties, she began to collect specimens and volunteered to reorganize the academy's herbarium. When the position of curator of botany became vacant, she accepted the offer but continued her field work, and was soon joined in specimen collecting by Townshend Stith Brandegee, who turned out to be that rarity, the perfect mate: their honeymoon was spent botanizing the whole length of a 500-mile walk.

After the Brandegees persuaded botanist Alice Eastwood to join and eventually replace them at the academy, the couple indulged in a mutual dream. Retiring on independent means, they devoted their time to collecting, and such was their reputation that many new finds in the field of botany were named for this now eminent pair of plant discoverers. Although Kate never wrote the flora of California she had planned, her impact was felt nonetheless. She had established the model for women to be taken seriously as professional botanists.

These professionals subsequently organized and administered specimen collections, researched, wrote, and taught, and certainly collected. Alice Eastwood was one of them.

One of the few shining moments in Alice's difficult, shifting childhood must have been her tutelage in botany by a fond uncle. She continued the study of botany on her own after she finished high school, when she was immediately pressed into teaching children just a little younger than herself. But summers were all hers. She used the time to explore and collect in the Rockies beyond her Denver home while trying to become a full-time botanist. She certainly succeeded; in 1892, when she was thirty-three years old, she got the invitation from the Brandegees to come to San Francisco as co-curator of the California Academy of Sciences herbarium.

She was editing the botany publication, running the herbarium, and adding to it with her own collecting in 1906 when the San Francisco earthquake struck. With a fire raging in a nearby building, she managed to save 1,200 specimens, then started all over again to collect what had been lost. She ultimately added a heroic 340,000 specimens to the academy herbarium, which was rebuilt in 1912 with Alice again at the helm.

Although she retired officially in 1949 when she was ninety, she continued to work at her desk. The following year she was made honorary president of the International Botanical Congress. The annual meeting was held in Sweden, where, fittingly, the accomplished nonagenarian was honored with the ultimate salute: she was seated in the almost sacred chair of Carolus Linnaeus.

Alice was not alone among women botanists who not only survived but continued to work into their nineties. Was it the hardy outdoor life they led much of the time? Or their lively commitment to work? Or the variety of activities and demands that kept their minds as well as bodies agile into old age? The study has yet to be done.

Some of the women botanists specialized in a particular geographical area, as both Kates did, collecting a wide range of specimens within a locale, whether it was a place as concentrated as the pine barrens of New Jersey (Mary Treat) or as vast as Mexico and much of South America (Ynes Mexia). Others added greatly to the depth and breadth of a single large sub-

Kate Brandegee on mule-back, heading out on a botanizing expedition to the mountains from San Jose del Cabo, California. Courtesy University and Jepson Herbaria, University of California, Berkeley.

ject. Agnes Chase was famous within the botanical world as an authority on grasses. Elizabeth Gertrude Knight Britton decided on a field that in the late Victorian era was inhabited rather thinly by researchers. She became a bryologist, studying mosses, liverworts, and other nonflowering plants.

Elizabeth's interest in plants came early; by her mid-twenties she was being praised by other professional botanists for her discoveries and her unusual acuity in this daunting area. It was mutual good fortune that Elizabeth ended up marrying a fellow botanist, Nathaniel Lord Britton, who valued her work and her abilities but was happy to leave the mosses and liverworts to his wife; he was interested in flowers.

After a trip to the Royal Gardens at Kew, the couple decided the equivalent was needed in New York, and engineered an appeal in 1889. Columbia College, where Nathaniel researched and taught botany, pledged

its herbarium and a sizable sum of money. The project won both municipal and private funds, and attracted a stellar board of directors that included philanthropist Andrew Carnegie, financier J. Pierpont Morgan, and Seth Low, president of Columbia College. Nathaniel was appointed director of the institution in 1896, and the garden opened officially in 1902. At no extra cost, the enterprise also got Elizabeth who worked alongside her husband while she continued to write and collect. In 1934, full of accomplishments and the pleasure of a life's work shared, the pair died within four months of one another.

The commitment that was evident in all these women's lives seems to have been possible in the nineteenth century under two conditions: marrying exactly the right man, or not marrying at all. None of the botanists in this account had children (even though some had been married before their careers began).

Alice Eastwood collects in the field with plant press at the ready and a clutch of her namesake grass, *Festuca eastwoodae*, in hand. Courtesy Special Collection Department, California Academy of Sciences, San Francisco.

Plants were their children—and sometimes their primary companions.

Botanizing was a socially acceptable way of having a remarkably adventurous career, and of traveling widely, not only to other American cities or abroad but of going to places unthinkable for a woman, accompanied perhaps only by a native guide or two. Agnes Chase was one of those botanical adventurers. Born in 1869, she had a hard childhood in which school was an indulgence she was briefly permitted, while work was a necessity forced upon her immediately after grammar school. At age nineteen, she married the editor of a small education periodical. Her husband died of tuberculosis within the year. Agnes rolled up her sleeves and doubled her work load to pay off his debts.

A growing interest in botany was furthered by creating illustrations of mosses for a botanist, who taught Agnes what he knew, and by 1903 she had be-

come good enough to be hired as an illustrator by the United States Department of Agriculture. Drawn to agrostology, the study of grasses, she worked after-hours in the department's herbarium learning her subject.

Her first scientific paper on grasses was published in 1906, and a great deal more writing, as well as professional promotions within the USDA followed. In 1922, she made her first tour of a number of European herbaria, consulting with other scientists and enjoying her recognition. Two years later, on her first collecting trip to South America, she endured remarkable physical challenges and eventually brought back thousands of specimens from Brazil and Venezuela, including newly discovered species.

Retirement in 1939 was a mere formality. Only the arduous field trips stopped; Agnes continued working in every aspect of her profession, as well as encouraging young botanists, and receiving honor upon

Ynes Mexia lived in this primitive thatched hut for three months while collecting plants in Amazonia, Peru. Courtesy University and Jepson Herbaria, University of California, Berkeley.

honor until 1963, when she turned ninety-five. She died five months after stopping.

The courage and physical resilience of these women botanists seems remarkable in any century. Once they had left civilization, they traveled by horse, mule, wagon, on rafts, in dugout canoes, and of course on foot. Sometimes they spent months botanizing, living in primitive conditions from tents to cots on the open ground to rest huts so filthy they had to be shoveled out before they could serve as dubious shelters. And nothing kept them from being eaten alive by swarms of flying insects. The insects were ignored.

They were also signally resourceful—building an instant raft when there was no other way to get to the middle of a pond for a specimen; waiting calmly for rescue on a narrow ledge above a ravine; improvising sleeping quarters and bathing facilities with whatever

was at hand; and supplementing their basic provender with chance bartering and random hospitality.

Ynes Mexia seemed to adapt instantly to the wilderness. During her first collecting trip to the far reaches of Mexico in 1925, she "got out her canoe [and] pulled her boots off and waded in the warm, shallow water. Soft mud oozed up between her toes and she felt beautifully enclosed in a world of blue water lilies and vine-covered trees while all around her flashed the brightly colored tropical birds" (Bonta, 106).

Ynes Mexia's earlier adult life was not much better than her difficult childhood. She was dogged by mental illness until late middle age. Then she turned to the study of botany, and it seems to have saved her. In long, adventurous journeys through Mexico, and later Brazil, Peru, and Ecuador, eaten up by insects and living and traveling under the most rudimentary conditions, she seemed to have found exactly the right

The botanical history of this little grass is remarkable! Nuttall first named and described it nearly thirty years ago; and while he referred it to *Sesleria*, suspected it to be *sui generis*, and threw out a happy conjecture as to its natural relationship. Torrey figured it twelve years ago, and also announced its affinity to the *Chlorideae*; he at the same time discovered its dioecious character, and showed that only the male plant was known. At length, Dr. Engelmann [of St. Louis], has detected the female plant in a rather rare grass, the *Anthephora axilliflora* of Steubel, which is so unlike the common Buffalo Grass that it naturally has been referred to a widely different tribe—struck by the similarity of their stoloniferous growth. Dr. Engelmann shrewdly suspected the relationship, and finally [found] a male Buffalo Grass which happened to bear a stalk of female flowers from the same root-stock; and these flowers

were those of the so-called *Anthophora*. So different are the two that nothing short of this ocular proof would have been convincing. Dr. Engelmann having to characterize this new generic type very naturally named it *Buchloe* (shorter and more euphonious than *Bubaloch loe*,) i.e. Buffalo Grass. It is curious to remark that the male plant being more proliferous by stolons than the female has nearly displaced the latter, or has (so far as known) attained a wider geographical range as well as a far greater abundance.

Abridged from Dr. Asa Gray's review of Dr. Engelmann's Report in 1859.

Dr. Gray's Papers. v. I. p. 112.

Buchloe dactyloides. Engelman.
Buffalo Grass.

Oak Creek, Nebraska—
June 4. 1888. J. W. Williams.

milieu for her sense of enterprise and her unstoppable energy. She botanized much of the time on her own, but occasionally with colleagues, among them Alice Eastwood, with whom she got on well, and Agnes Chase, with whom she did not.

She thought of herself as a risk-taking person with a job to do (she sold her specimens to a variety of scientific institutions to pay her expenses). But on that job, in that brief time, she collected hundreds of thousands of specimens that included many new species. On her last trip, even though already ill, she brought back thirteen thousand specimens from a rugged journey through Mexico, less than two months before her death.

Specimens were gathered from the two American continents in the thousands, ultimately the tens of thousands, by these courageous and determined women. They also gave their lives over to something larger than themselves, its evidence before their eyes. To ride out into the wilderness and be at home in it, find your work waiting there for you, must have given them a great sense of exhilaration. And yet, they were also at the center of civilization in its most cultivated forms.

opposite: Botanical specimen. Buffalo grass with extensive hand-written caption by its collector J. W. Williams, Nebraska, 1888. 16½ x 11½ in.

overleaf: Pages of multiple botanical specimens, each with a typeset caption, from *Plantes des Pyrénées,* a herbarium compiled in 1867. 18 x 12 in.

Heaven in Wildflowers

In the first half of the nineteenth century there was widespread belief among botanists that pursuit of the subject—and of natural history, generally—led to an understanding of God's universal plan. Textbooks emphasized a natural theology that raised the mind to God through contemplation of His designs. "His pencil grows in every flower," ran a popular aphorism.

Such beliefs were not necessarily inimical to the ideas presented by *On the Origin of Species,* in which Darwin proposed mutation of species through natural selection. Asa Gray supported Darwin while remaining committed to natural theology, and his many textbooks for children reflect this.[11] Science, it was believed, used understanding and reason, but also imagination to "decipher God's universal laws" and was "literally demonstrating heaven in wildflowers (Ladd 1968, 159).

Theories of art were also imbued with spiritual values. Romanticism, which embraced both art and literature, exalted the symbolic and allegorical power of the beauties of the natural world. In the romantic view, nature became a spiritual treasury and "the greatest record of human virtues" (Ladd, 167). In a treatise on the metamorphosis of plants, the German writer Johann Wolfgang von Goethe (1749–1832), a major exponent of romanticism, wrote that the sheer beauty of nature rendered it inaccessible to ordinary scientific proce

[11]Later in the century, in an effort to interest children in botany, a number of writers presented an anthropomorphic view of the nature of plants. *The Sagacity and Morality of Plants: A Sketch of the Life and Conduct of the Vegetable Kingdom,* published in 1891, declared that "The desire to found a family is as manifest among plants as among men!" Plants were shown to exhibit talents for walking (the Walking Fern) and even eating (the carnivorous plants) in *The Human Side of Plants,* published in New York in 1914.

HELIANTHEMUM ALPESTRE DC.
Penna-Blanca. — Juillet.

CISTUS SALVIÆFOLIUS L.
St-Béat. Juin.

HELIANTHEMUM RHODANTUM Dun.
St-Aventin. — Juin.

HELIANTHEMUM GRANDIFLORUM DC.
Rochers de Barcugnas. — Juin.

HELIANTHEMUM PILOSELLOIDES Lap.
Céciré. — Juillet.

HELIANTHEMUM POLIFOLIUM DC.
Antignac. Juin.

Silène Boulei gris
Boulest E. Jenesquise

SILENE SAXIFRAGA L.
Esquierry. — Juin.

SILENE RUPESTRIS L.
Vallée de Luchon. Juillet.

SILENE ACAULIS L.
Port de Venasque. — Juillet.

Silene gallica L.
Luchon juin.

SILENE ALPINA Thomas.
Esquierry. Juillet.

Silene procumbens Nod.
maladetta ili.

Silene nutans L.
Esquerr. juin.

dures, and that the highest artistic expression required a profound understanding of the flower and its mode of growth so that its inmost essence could be expressed visually (Ritterbush 1968, 5). A treatise by Goethe's contemporary Carl Gustav Carus (1789–1869), a professor of anatomy in Dresden, proposed the plant form as a symbol of human sensibility, with its roots in the unconscious and its stems and flowers reaching toward the Divine (Ritterbush, 13). The poet Samuel Taylor Coleridge (1772–1834) invoked the plant in his definition of organic form, which stated that the process of growth should be apparent in the form, as in the "evolution and extension in the Plant" (Ritterbush, 21). What better exemplar of these views than botanical specimens, in which art, science, and nature are combined in a single organic whole?

To what extent spiritual concerns actually influenced the botanizers is open to conjecture. We do know that scientific rigor was encouraged: botanical handbooks, such as *The Fern Collector's Guide* by Willard N. Clute, published in New York in 1901, were sternly practical in their instructions. "No specimen should be collected without carefully noting upon the sheet...the locality in which it was collected," wrote Clute. "If the name of a fern is lost, the plant can easily be identified again, but once the data regarding the locality is lost, it is gone forever. Specimens without locality are absolutely worthless."

Judging from the specimens found today, this admonishment was not consistently heeded. From the evidence, it seems that the joys of botanizing out-

weighed its rigors. Publications like *Harper's Young People* urged children to botanize and observe the beauties of their collections, as in an article on seaweeds in an August 1891 issue. "Many of the delicate weeds are so thin, and the colors are so vivid," writes the author, "that to an inexperienced eye they look more like figures in paint than actual plants."

Both ferns and seaweeds were favorites of botanizers. In England, as we have seen, the passion for ferns developed into a craze; but on both sides of the Atlantic, and along the Pacific Coast, seaweed was collected with just as much enthusiasm. The slithery plants would seem unsuited to pressing. In the nineteenth century, the common name was sea moss, or, more correctly, marine algae (experts in the subject are algologists). It was very difficult to harvest seaweed and prepare it for pressing and mounting, as is demonstrated in A. B. Harvey's popular guide *Sea Mosses*, published in Boston in 1881, a portion of which is reprinted as Appendix B (see page 141). When properly mounted, seaweeds are perhaps the most astonishingly beautiful of all botanical specimens, amazing in their varieties and colors. What was once slimy vegetable matter becomes a roseate veil, a puff of green, a spidery drawing.

The creators of seaweed herbaria often used a variety of plant forms to make pictures that could range from a simple ribbon garland to a complex and elaborately designed Victorian memorial picture—George

opposite: A page from a Victorian herbarium inscribed with a poem and mounted with specimens representing "Love in Idleness," "Distinction," and "Fascination."

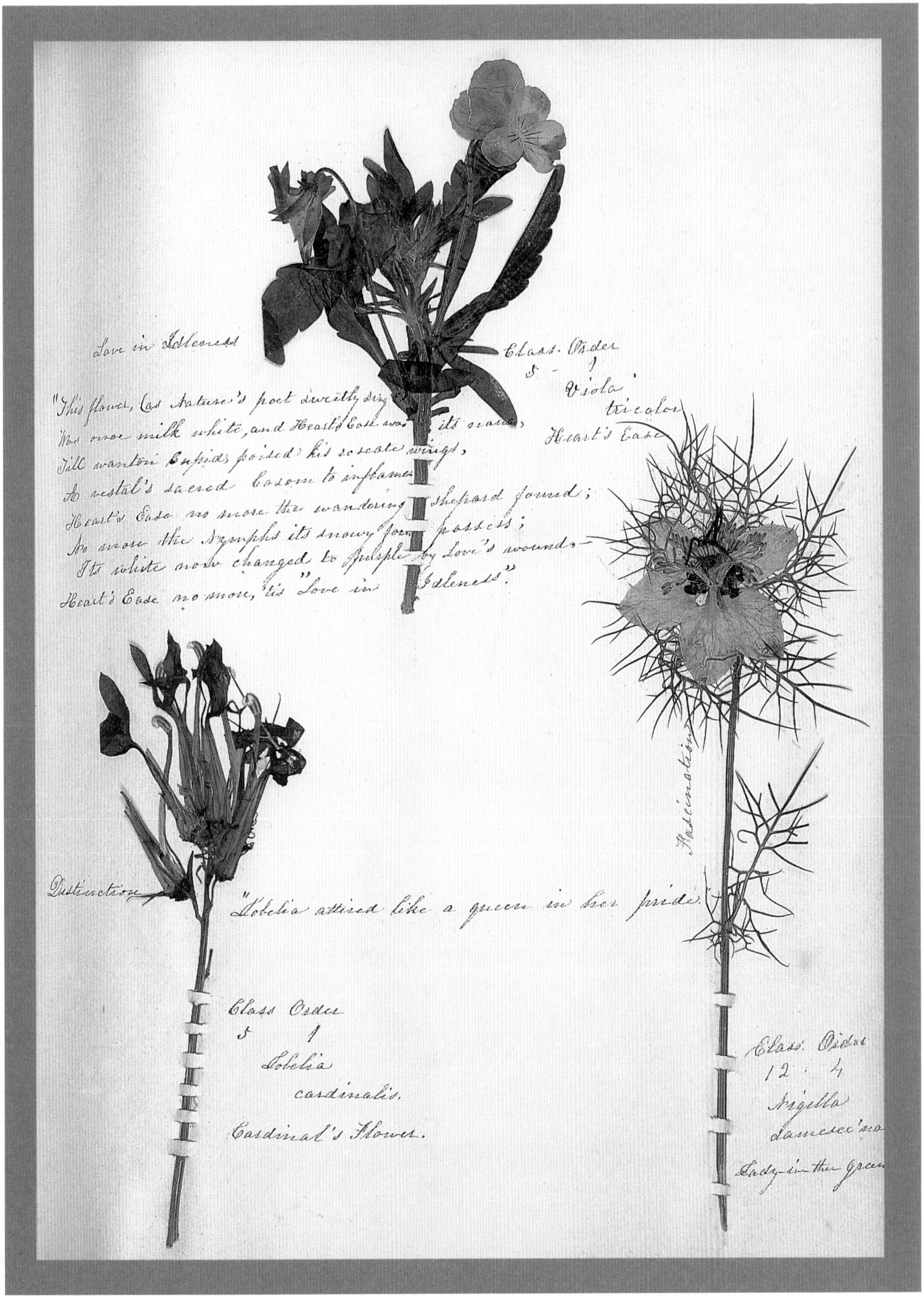

Love in Idleness

"This flower, (as Nature's poet sweetly sing)
Was once milk white, and Heart's Ease was its name;
Till wanton Cupids poised his roseate wings,
A vestal's sacred bosom to inflame
Heart's Ease no more the wandering shepard found;
No more the Nymphs its snowy form possess;
Its white now changed to purple by Love's wound—
Heart's Ease no more, 'tis "Love in Idleness"

Class. Order
5 - 1
Viola
tricolor
Heart's Ease

Distinction

"Lobelia attired like a queen in her pride."

Fascination

Class Order
5   1
Lobelia
cardinalis.
Cardinal's Flower.

Class. Order
12 . 4
Nigella
damasce'na
Lady-in-the-Green

Gaadea luminaroides

above and opposite: Specimens of a variety of unidentified seaweeds. American, nineteenth century.

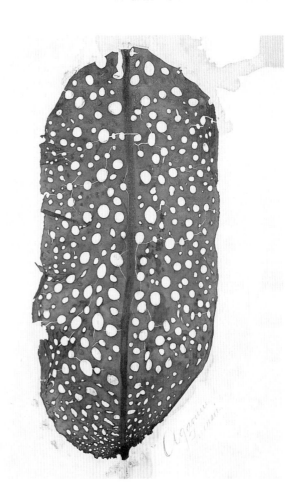

Washington's tomb, for example, complete with obelisk and weeping willows (page 26).

Given the time and effort it took to create a herbarium, it may seem curious that examples found today are often anonymous, dated perhaps, but unsigned. There are exceptions, such as the minimal inscription found in a bound album of Darjeeling ferns, prepared by an Elizabeth E. Hawkins and dated April 1882, which states that the plants were "mounted by Mrs. P. Jaffrey."

We must imagine the details: Elizabeth Hawkins might have been the wife of a British colonialist stationed in India during the heyday of the Raj. She fills her time, between afternoon teas and diplomatic dinners, with plant collecting and is aided in the creation of a herbarium by a Mrs. Jaffrey, who agrees to take on the task. Or Elizabeth may have been a romantic young woman whose forays into the fern-laden forests were an excuse to meet a lover. Whatever the story, the herbarium—which contains a remarkable collection of about forty ferns—has kept the secret for over a hundred years.

In some cases, anonymity may have been accidental, caused possibly when a page was lost in rebinding. This is most likely the case with a two-volume eighteenth-century herbarium found in London, a small portion of which is reproduced on pages 80–89. Unsigned, but precisely dated "April 25, 1798" on the last page of the first volume, it is remarkable for its

this page and opposite: Specimens from an oversized album of Darjeeling ferns, signed "Elizabeth E. Hawkins, April 15, 1882." 8 x 12 in.

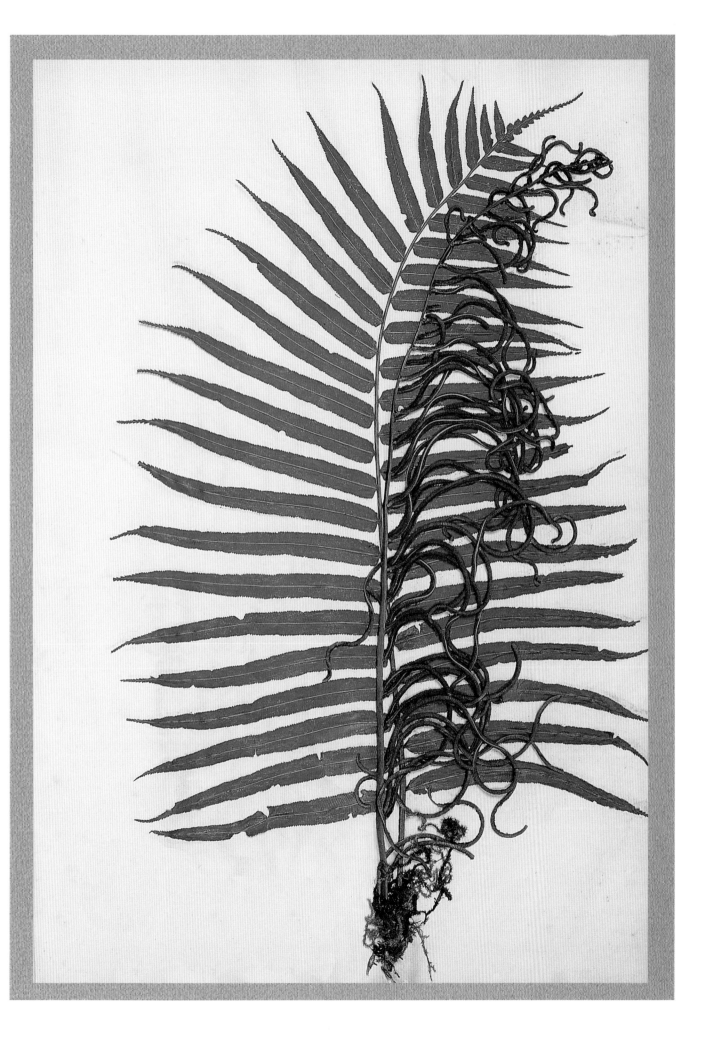

blending of science, art, nature, and writing. Quaintly titled *Specimens of British Plants Collected in their Native Soils with their Classical, Generical, and Specifical distinctions and Occasional Remarks*, it carries a title page with an excerpt from *The Botanic Garden*, a famous poem written in 1792 by Erasmus Darwin, Charles Darwin's grandfather. A brief excerpt from the poem quoted in the herbarium reads:

> Lo! on each Seed within its slender rind
> Lifes golden threads in endless circles wind;
> Maze within maze the lucid webs are roll'd,
> And, as they burst, the living flames unfold.

Page after page of minute, delicate script conveys the author's impressive knowledge of plants and folklore in often lengthy captions. After the plant names, collecting locales are given, sometimes so precisely that they could be found today: *"From a hedge between Melton & Witford bridge (Suffolk) Aug. between Stow market and Gripping (Suffolk)"* Now and then a wry wit creeps into captions, as in one for *Pisum Maritimim*, the sea pea collected in Allborough, Suffolk: *"It is reported, that the people in this neighborhood were preserved from death in the year 1555, a year of famine! by gathering the seeds of this plant & eating them as food. In a like urgency, [people today] must not expect similar relief, a small portion of plants being now found on that coast, only food sufficient for the hungry botanist."*

Sadly, the author's identity is forever lost to us, a page bearing his or her name perhaps having been cut off when the herbarium was rebound in green leather with a gold-stamped red spine. We can be grateful, though, that in the two hundred years since this herbarium was made, the specimens were kept intact and in proper sequence so that, in what can only be called inspired—if accidental—design, the pressed plant faces its mirror-image stain on each opposing page, as if the plant's shadow has been cast over the writing.

In much the same way, the shadows of the great plant hunters and the avid amateur botanizers are cast over all of botanical history. Their stories, only briefly sketched here, give merely a faint idea of how much contemporary gardeners and plant enthusiasts owe to their heroic efforts. Botanical specimens provide a tangible link to them and the plants they sometimes risked their lives to collect.

above: Handwritten title page from a rare eighteenth-century herbarium of British plants, with part of a one-hundred-line poem by Erasmus Darwin. Additional examples of pages from this extraordinary album, some with transcribed captions, follow on pages 81–89.

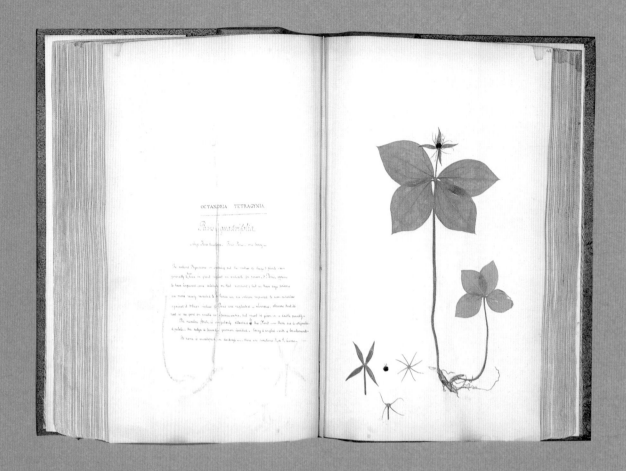

OCTANDRIA TETRAGYNIA
Paris quadrifolia
Ang: Herb truelove —Herb Paris—one berry

*The ancient Physicians in seeking out the virtues of drugs & plants seem
generally to have had in great request an antidote for poison, & Paris, appears
to have acquired some celebrity on that account; but in these days poisons are
more rarely resorted to & hence we are seldom required to arm ourselves
against it. These virtues of Paris are neglected—Linnaeus, observes that its root
is as good an emetic as Ipecacuantra, but must be given in a double quantity.
 The number four, is singularly attached to this plant—there are
4 stigmata—4 petals—the calyx 4 leaved—german 4 sided—berry 4 angled—
with 4 loculaments—The name is enveloped in darkness—there are sometimes
3, or 5, leaves.*

PENTANDRIA DIGYNIA
Lanicula Europaea
Ang. Lanicle

Woods & shady places—May–June
A French proverb says, "He who is possessed of Lanicle and
Bugle, may dismiss his surgeons" but modern practice does
not countinance [sic] such an assertion—W.

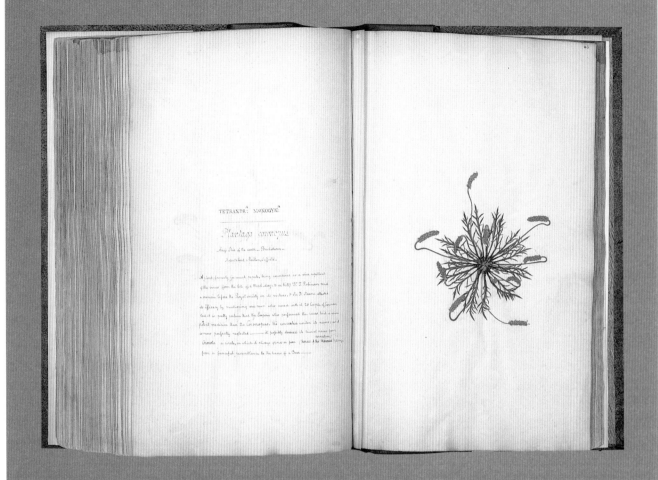

TETANDRIA: MONOGYNIA

Plantago cornopus

Ang: Star of the earth—buckshorn

Hab: about Melton, Suffolk
A plant formerly in much repute, being considered as a sure repellant of the virus
from the bite of a Mad dog: & in 1687, Dr. T. Robinson read a memoir before the
Royal society on its virtues, & Sir H. Sloane attested its efficacy by mentioning one
man who cured with it 20 Couple of hounds: but it is pretty certain that the
Empiric who performed the cures had a more potent medicinal than the Coronopsus,
tho concealed under its name; as it is now perfectly neglected—it possibly derived its
trivial name from coronata, a circle in which it always grows or from (keras) cornu-
tum, horny, from a fanciful resemblance to the horns of a Deer.

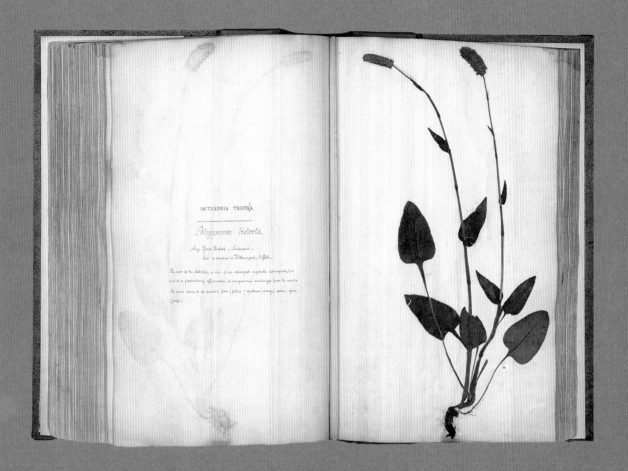

OCTANDRIA TRIGYNIA
Polygonum bistorta
Ang: Great Bistort—Snakeweed

Hab: A meadow in Witheringset, Suffolk—
The root of the bistorta, is one of our strongest vegetable
astringents, & is said to be particularly efficaceous in san-
guinous discharges from the viscera. Its name seems to be
derived from (polus) multum (many) gonu, genu (joints).

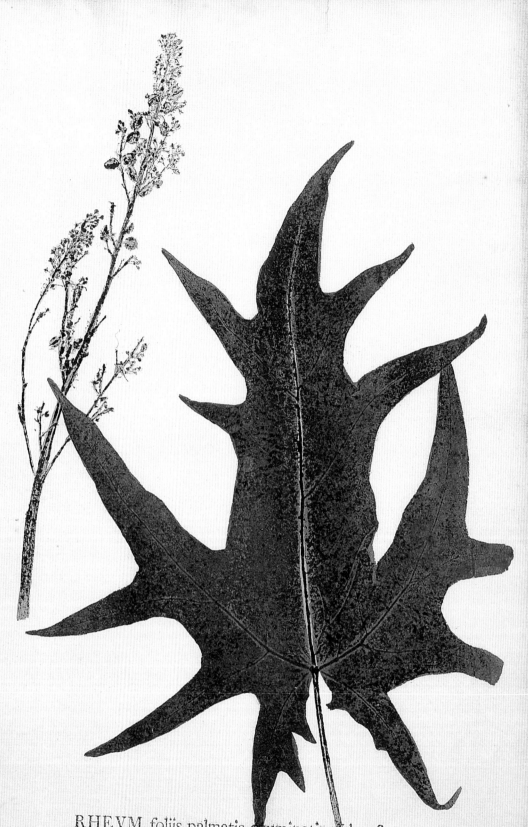

RHEVM foliis palmatis acuminatis. *Linn. spec.* 2. 531.
Ludw. D. G. P. 194.
- - - palmatum.

the plant's
impression

The seemingly fanciful notion of a picture that draws itself is at the heart of both nature printing and photography. Both are in fact modes of reproduction in which the subject can create its own image. Nature printing seemed an improvement on drawings or paintings, which tended to be either too generalized or too idealized; and it offered the possibility of printing in multiples. Photography would fulfill that promise, but, in its earliest form, the sun picture, which used real plants to make hazy impressions on paper, seemed more akin to magic than practicality. Today, both nature prints and sun pictures are appreciated more as art than science, and yet they retain their links to both.

opposite: Nature print. *Rheum.* from *Botanica in Originali* by Hieranymous Kniphof, 1764. $12^3/_4$ x $7^3/_4$ in.

nature
prints "And Flow'rs themselves were taught to paint."

—Andrew Marvell, The Mower Against Gardens

Nature print. A leaf's veins and serrated edge are perfectly reproduced in this anonymous hand-colored print inscribed *Hibiscus esculentus*.

LIKE A FINGERPRINT, a nature print is, at its simplest, a stamped image that results when an object, such as a leaf or an entire plant, is coated with ink and pressed to paper. The resulting image is an amalgam of elemental beauty and realism of an almost microscopic quality. Within a crisp outline, each nature-printed leaf reveals not only its own unique shape but its intricate system of veining with every minute imperfection. These are micro-details largely beyond the powers of art. Nature-printed plants are perfect replications, exactly the same size as the plant and complete with translucent petals, hairy stems, and knotty roots, ap-

pearing as if freshly picked from the earth. Quite understandably, more than a few botanists turned to nature printing in search of a method for creating accurate visual records of plants. They knew that although skillful draftmanship could produce a satisfactory, even diagrammatic, rendering of a plant, it was just no substitute for the real thing.

Nature printing had precursors in stone and metal rubbings of classical antiquity. Examples also appear in non-Western textile decoration, such as Tahitian bark cloth, which was printed with fern and hibiscus leaves that had been dipped in red sap and pressed to the fabric (Danielsson 1966, 85).

The first use of nature printing in botanical texts has been traced back as far as A.D. 1229 (Heilmann, June 1995) A Syrian manuscript of Dioscorides's early *De Materia Medica*, now in the library of the Topkapi Museum in Istanbul, is illustrated with impressions of whole plants that were then hand colored in green. Another early example, dating from 1425, is the Italian travel diary of a physician, Conrad von Butzbach, who coated leaves with various colored inks and printed them directly into his notebook. This example predates, by sixty to one hundred years, Leonardo da Vinci's better-known illustration and explanation of nature printing in the *Codex Atlanticus,* folio 72, verso 2, in Milan's Biblioteca Ambrosiana. Produced sometime between 1490 and 1519, the text contains da Vinci's explanation of how a sage leaf coated with lamp black and oil could be printed.

A number of sixteenth-century herbalists and printers experimented with nature printing, using a variety of inking substances from verdigris and carbon to oil and soot. Among them was Alexis Pedemontanus, who, in his book *Liber de Secretis Naturae* (Secrets of Nature), published in Milan in 1557, described medical and alchemical recipes, including one for nature printing that advised the rather dubious procedure of bruising a leaf before coating it with a mixture of linseed oil and soot, then pressing it "lightly down with your hand" between sheets of paper. The resulting prints, which could be dyed green according to another recipe, were termed by him "gallant things, to adorne your Chamber." Zenobius Pacinus, a Florentine spice dealer famous for a longevity potion, made nature prints of the

medicinal ingredients he used, which included plants and vipers. He thus became the first person known to have made an animal nature print (Heilmann, June 1995). Antoine Mizauld proposed using skeletonized leaves to best show a plant's structure, an approach that would be used to great effect in the nineteenth century.

The first mention of the use of printer's ink and a press in connection with nature printing occurs in a 1687 text by a J. D. Geyer, who described a process in which a leaf could be smeared with printer's ink, then "with the assistance of a press or screw [could be printed] onto a slightly moistened sheet of paper [with the result that] a more accurate image could hardly be produced" (Cave and Wakeman 1967, 7). The method was highly recommended as "extremely useful to those botanists who have no artistic talent, as by these elegant means they can prepare an herbarium themselves."

Nature printing was probably introduced into England in the early seventeenth century by a Cistercian monk named Silvio Boccone, who made two major print compilations (Heilmann, September 1995) and shared the knowledge with the botanist William Sherard, among others. One of the first known nature printers in America was a German lawyer, Francis Daniel Pastorius, who immigrated in 1683 with a group of fellow Quakers. The group, called the Company of Frankfurt, founded Germantown, now a part of Philadelphia (Harris 1989). A book heavily decorated with Pastorius's nature prints, Michael Pexenfelder's *Apparatus Eruditionis* (see page 94) is in the collection of the Library Company of Philadelphia. That same institution, founded by Benjamin Franklin,

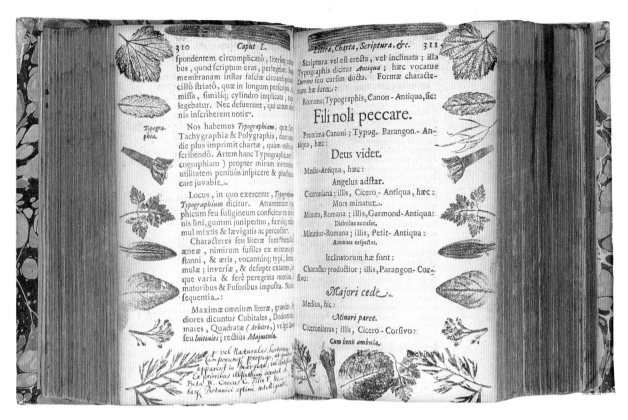

Leaf prints by Francis Daniel Pastorius, a German émigré to America, adorn Michael Pexenfelder's eighteenth-century *Apparatus Eruditionis*.

also has examples of leaf prints made by the Philadelphia engraver Joseph Breintnall, who was a friend of both Pastorius and Franklin.

In France, a nature-printed manuscript record of the plants in the Jardin Royal in Paris was made by Jean de la Hire. A German pharmacist, Johann Georg Schmidt, made nature prints of enormous size using lengths of folded paper. One, which has not survived, was a sunflower that measured about 13 feet from flower to root.

A fine example of eighteenth-century nature-printed book illustration was produced by Hieronymus Kniphof, a professor and librarian of the botanical society of the city of Erfurt, who created prints in partnership with bookseller/publisher J. M. Funcken. *Botanica in Originali se Herbarium Vivum* (see pages 96–98) was published between about 1728 and 1764 in three volumes devoted, respectively, to medici-

nal and pharmaceutical plants, vegetables, and garden plants. Kniphof was uniquely skilled at making nature prints of round and rounded objects, like cabbage heads or root vegetables, but never divulged his secret. The plates are notable for the clarity of the impressions, the variety of the plants illustrated, and, in later editions, the quality of the hand coloring. In a comparison of different editions, we can see that Kniphof replaced plants as they became worn out from printing—similar species were used, but sometimes in different stages of growth. It was planned that the work would be published in "centuries"—editions of a hundred plates each—but only three manuscripts of 1,200 prints each were completed (Heilmann, December 1995). The definitive edition of *Botanica in Originali* was published between 1757 and 1764, the year after Kniphof died. Approximately fourteen copies of this edition were made. It was finished by F. W. Leyser and

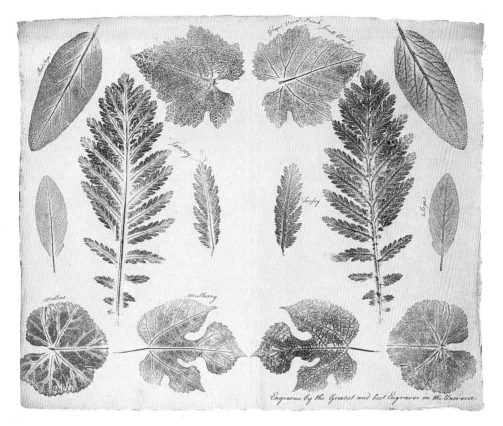

A page of direct nature prints skillfully made by the Philadelphia engraver Joseph Breintnall shows both backs and fronts of a variety of leaves. The print bears Brientnall's usual declaration: "Engraved by the Greatest and best engraver in the Universe." Library Company of Philadelphia.

contained 1,200 plates. With so few editions made, *Botanica in Originali* was extremely rare even in its own time. (One sold at auction in 1811 for about the same price as a Gutenberg Bible.[12])

For all its virtues, nature printing had a major weakness. A plant or leaf would not hold up indefinitely, and after several inkings and stampings it would fall apart from use. So "editions" such as Kniphof's were severely limited. Clearly, an alternative to the direct-print method was needed, one that could transfer the plant's impression to a printing plate. Logic dictated this crucial step: taking a mold of the plant's impression from which a printing plate could be made.

A truly workable method would be found in the nineteenth century, but until then, printers—independently of one another—worked toward creating an acceptable mold. They tried a variety of substances, including plaster of Paris, isinglass, and the natural plastic gutta-percha, but all of these proved problematic. One ingenious solution came from an unlikely place—the American colonies—where Benjamin Franklin concentrated his prodigious mind on foiling counterfeiters by incorporating nature prints of leaves into paper currency designs (see pages 100–103). There is no evidence that Franklin's secret method ever crossed the Atlantic.

[12] *Botanica in Originali* was brought to Japan in 1823 by the German physician and botanist Phillip Franz Balthasar von Siebold. He shared it with Japanese botanists who thereafter developed an intense interest in nature printing and produced numerous examples (Heilmann 1990).

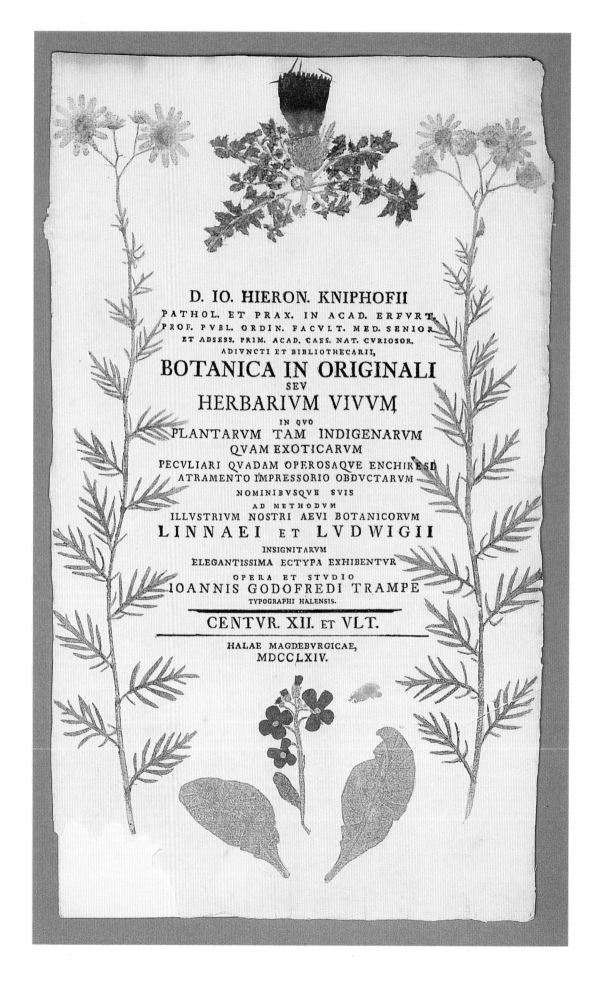

pages 96–99: Pages from the nature-printed portfolio *Botanica in Originali* with title page, above. 12¾ x 7¾.

GNAPHALIVM herbaceum, foliis lineari-lanceolatis
acuminatis alternis, caule fuperne ramofo,
corymbis faftigiatis. *Linn. fpec.* 2. 1198.
Ludw. D. G. P. 403.
- - - - - margaritaceum.

MELIANTHVS ſtipulis ſolitariis petiolo adnatis.
Linn. ſpec. 2. 892. *Ludw.* D. G. P. 605.
‐ ‐ ‐ ‐ ‐ ‐ ‐ maior.

HELIANTHVS foliis omnibus cordatis trineruatis,
floribus cernuis. *Linn. fpec.* 2. 1276.
Ludw. D. G. P. 466.
- - - - - - annuus.

ben franklin's leaf:
a mystery story

Benjamin Franklin developed a colonial currency design that held a secret known only to a handful of his printer friends, and it remained unknown for well over two hundred years. Paper currency with a variety of ornamental designs had been printed in the American colonies since 1690. When Franklin was engaged by the Pennsylvania Assembly to print currency, he was keenly aware that the bills were highly susceptible to counterfeiting. The problem was that no matter how intricate the design, what one man could create and engrave, another could copy.

He was also acquainted with the unusual technique of printing a few impressions directly from a botanical specimen. It was a technique being employed by Franklin's friend Joseph Breintnall, a Philadelphia botanist and engraver who by the 1730s had turned out more than a hundred nature prints, which he sold for scientific purposes. Franklin himself produced a nature print of a leaf of the rattlesnake plant (goldenrod) in his *Poor Richard's Almanac* in 1737. It struck him that an improved method of nature printing was the way to foil counterfeiting.

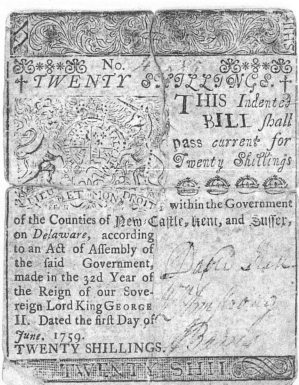

top and bottom: Front and back of a 1759 twenty-shilling note, with nature-printed leaf.

But couldn't the improved nature-printed leaf be copied by a good engraver? The answer to this and other puzzling questions began to surface in Philadelphia some 224 years after Franklin introduced the first nature-printed colonial bills on August 10, 1739.

An exhibition of floral art was to be presented by the Philadelphia Museum of Art in 1963. While working on the exhibition and catalog, Whitfield J. Bell, Jr., associate editor of *The Papers of Benjamin Franklin,* asserted that Franklin's leaf-patterned currency—used by Franklin through much of the eighteenth century—in fact held nature-printed images that involved stereotype transfers from real leaves, not engravings. Cart Zigrosser and Kneeland McNulty, curator and associate curator, respectively, of the museum's print department, looked into this suggestion and published their findings in the exhibition catalog (1963). But an impenetrable mystery still remained: why and how was it done?

Eric P. Newman, along with Whitfield Bell, was asked if he would be willing to undertake a thorough inves-

Nature-printed colonial currency produced by Benjamin Franklin aimed to thwart counterfeiters. All courtesy of Eric P. Newman.

tigation. Newman is a now-retired lawyer and expert numismatist. His findings were published serially in four issues of *The Numismatist* in the winter and spring of 1964. Newman determined, after assiduous detective work, that hand-engraved leaf designs were no more of a foil to counterfeiters than "any other complex design." There had to be something else about leaf patterns that gave Franklin's botanicals the advantage for decades on colonial currency. And indeed Franklin printed a transfer from the leaf itself.

"Franklin must have realized from Breintnall's leaf prints and otherwise," Newman wrote in the February 1964 issue, "that leaves not only had exceedingly complex detail but also that their internal lines were graduated in thickness. This would make virtually impossible a fine reproduction by engraving. If, therefore, Franklin could keep his nature printing process concealed, he would have a very effective weapon against counterfeiting."

The problem would end there, except that actual leaf subjects would wear out long before hundreds of thousands of currency bills were printed. But why not then just replace the tattered sample with a similar leaf? Because it was impractical and would engender monetary chaos to have new bills appear every few weeks with different designs, however subtle. And there is another advantage to printing from the leaf itself besides its three-dimensional complexity: the leaf's utter distinctiveness.

"Each leaf, like a fingerprint, has characteristics of its own, differing from every other leaf, whether on the same plant or of the same species," Newman pointed out in his series of articles.

Thus the final mystery: How do you take an impression of a leaf—clear and minutely detailed in all its breathtaking intricacy—without damaging it and produce a printing plate that works and is enduring? The technology that could have made this possible was still at least a hundred years off.

Newman suggests that a transfer of the print was required to make a mold into which type metal could then be poured to make a printing plate. "It seems logical," Newman wrote, "to assume that the process was as follows: Soft plaster was placed in a retainer and smoothed flat. Then a wet piece of textured fabric was laid on that surface. A moistened or fresh leaf then was laid onto the cloth, possibly with an adhesive or a film of plaster applied between them, so the leaf would adhere to the cloth after drying"

(Newman 1964, 305). Through pressure exerted by a "flat smooth board...the leaf was forced down into the portion of the cloth underneath the leaf. In this way the veins and other high detail of the leaf and the threads of the exposed cloth were forced to take the same horizontal level. This unit was permitted to harden in that position.

"To make a plaster negative of this unit merely required oiling the contact surface and applying a plaster mixture on top....The plaster negative, when hard, then would become a mold into which melted type metal could be poured to make a cut [engraved printing block or plate]. If the cut was withdrawn without harming the mold, additional cuts could be similarly cast, all of which would be identical. Thus...with care and skill a three-dimensional object of nature could be reproduced in detail upon one or more identical cuts for flat bed printing" (Newman, 305).

Until and unless altered by the discovery of some long lost document, this stands as a very plausible explanation. Franklin later shared the secret with a partner and then other currency printers. They all remained mum, and so the secret remained until the twentieth-century-Philadelphia discovery, and Eric Newman's subsequent detecting, adding yet another feather to Benjamin Franklin's prodigious cap.

opposite: Nature-printed leaves set in a baroque cartouche. Johann Michael Seligmann. *Die Nahrungs-Gefase in den Blattern der Baume.* Nuremberg, 1748. 17½ x 11½ in.

TAB. X.

Aranzo Incanitiato.

Nature Printing on the Press

In the first half of the nineteenth century, several individuals worked independently on a method for producing nature prints on a press. An intermediate step was required before a direct nature print could be transferred to a metal printing plate. In 1833, a Danish goldsmith, Peter Khyl, described placing a dried plant between two metal sheets, one of which was softened, and running both through a press to obtain a detailed impression.[13] In 1851, Dr. Ferguson Branson, an English physician, published the results of his experiments in printing from gutta-percha impressions of leaves. The result was unsatisfactory as the gutta-percha plate left smudges and fuzzy outlines on the prints. Branson then tried to create copperplates from the gutta-percha molds by means of electrotyping,[14] but he abandoned this process as too "tedious, troublesome, and costly" (Cave and Wakeman, 18).

Although Branson abandoned his research, his ideas on casting gutta-percha molds in metal most certainly inspired others. His methods, or variations thereof, may have been used, for example, by Nottingham lacemakers to produce printed pattern books. At any rate, it was printed lace samples exhibited at the Great Exhibition of 1851 in London that spurred advances in botanical nature printing. Included in the printing technology exhibit were examples of nature-printed lace and leaves produced by an English printer, William Taylor, from impressions made in metal. The delicate, intricately patterned lace specimens were brought to the attention of Alois Auer, director of the Imperial Printing House in Vienna, who in 1852 set his staff to work trying to obtain the same effect.

To make the initial impressions from real lace samples, Auer first tried gutta-percha.[15] The printing house overseer, Andrew Worring, substituted soft lead, which produced extremely fine lace impressions. When the director of the Imperial Geological Society, Wilhelm Haidinger, saw these impressions, he suggested using the same lead method to print plants, and the result was an unqualified success. Nature printing took a great leap forward, acquiring an impressive German name in

---

[13] The details of his method remained unknown until he published his manuscript in 1853. Khyl may have been inspired by an intaglio process known as siderography, brought to England from America in 1819 by a Jacob Perkins. It involved engraving a design directly on softened metal, which was then tempered and used as the printing plate. It became a standard method of printing banknotes and postage stamps in the 1850s.

[14] Electrotyping, invented in 1839, is a method of making a duplicate plate from a mold. It is an intermediate step in the copperplate printing process, commonly used in high-quality, high-volume printing, for embossed stationery, for example. The process involves first taking a wax mold of the object to be duplicated, such as an engraving, woodcut, or, in nature printing, a leaf or plant impression in soft metal. The wax mold is then coated with a substance, such as graphite, that acts as a conductor of electricity, and then immersed in a electrolytic chemical bath containing copper. An electrical charge causes the mold to be coated with a thin shell of copper. The shell, with its delicate relief impression, is removed from the mold and reinforced with a backing of lead alloy. This becomes the duplicate printing plate.

Naturselbstdruck.
Aus der k. k. Hof- und Staatsdruckerei zu Wien. 1853.

Electrotype nature print. Lace. Printed by Alois Auer. Vienna, Austria, 1853. 7 x 11¾ in.

the process. Auer called it *Naturselbstdruck*, which translates as "nature self-print," and in 1853 he delivered a lecture (published in 1854 in German, English, French, and Italian) describing the discovery: "An invention for creating by means of the original itself—in a swift and simple manner—plates for printing copies of plants, materials, lace...containing the most delicate profundities or elevations...in various colors with one single impression...by the ordinary letterpress [or] copperplate press...without the aid of drawing or engraving."

Auer's nature-printing process involved several steps: first the leaf (or plant) was pressed between soft-ened lead and a sheet of steel, leaving an impression in the lead. After removing the leaf, he made the electrotype copperplate. In 1853, the first book printed with Auer's process was published: a botanical work of forty-four nature prints of the flora of the Carpathian Mountains in Transylvania.

Although Auer patented the process, he did not intend to retain exclusive usage rights to it. Nonetheless, he felt proprietary about it, and was therefore angered to learn that in June 1853, the English printers William Bradbury and Frederick Evans had taken out a patent for "improvements" on basically the same

[15]Auer had used gutta-percha extensively to make plate molds of geological specimens, from which he obtained excellent nature prints. The process involved etching the face of the specimen, then taking an impression of it in gutta-percha, from which a print could be made. A method of taking direct prints from etched meteorites had been invented in Austria in the early nineteenth century. In 1845, Wilhelm Haidinger, director of the Imperial Geological Society, published handbooks illustrated with nature prints of geological specimens (Cave and Wakeman, 20). He may have used the gutta-percha technique in the printing process.

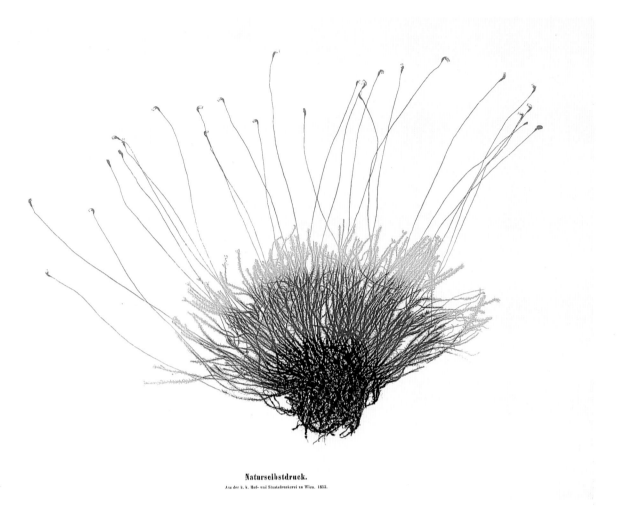

Naturselbstdruck.
Aus der k. k. Hof- und Staatsdruckerei zu Wien. 1853.

Electrotype nature print. Lichen. Printed by Alois Auer. Vienna, Austria. 1853. 13¼ x 10 in.

process—without mentioning his name. The ensuing feud had aspects of a tragicomedy. The news of Bradbury's patent came to him through William Bradbury's son, Henry, who had in fact spent several months in 1852 as Auer's guest, observing and learning various processes at the Imperial Printing Office. In January 1854, an incensed Auer fired off a publication in four languages entitled *The Conduct of a Young Englishman,* which accused Henry Bradbury not of piracy, but of poor conduct during his visit to the printing office. This consisted, maintained Auer, of drunkenness, as well as using bribery in an attempt to gain a set of prints from one of Auer's overseers. Whatever the truth of the matter, from that moment on, the English and

Austrians were pitted against each other, each maintaining their priority for discovering the process.

Henry Bradbury responded to *Conduct of a Young Englishman* with a lecture at the Royal Institution in 1855 that gave a detailed description and history of the process, including the electrotyping step, without mentioning Auer's name. When the lecture was published in 1856 under the title *Nature Printing: Its Origin and Objects,* a German translation—dedicated to Auer—was provided, perhaps as an obliquely offered olive branch.

In 1855, Auer and Bradbury each published masterpieces of nature printing. Auer's is the more ambitious: the five-volume *Physiotypia Plantarum Austria-*

Naturselbstdruck.

Aus der k. k. Hof- und Staatsdruckerei zu Wien. 1853.

Electrotype nature print. Flowers. Printed by Alois Auer. Vienna, Austria. 1853. 13¼ x 10 in.

carum of Constantin von Ettingshausen and Alois Pokorny. It was issued in an oversized 22- by 15-inch format and showed skeletonized leaves, considered the optimal method for botanical analysis of leaf venation. It was also a boon to the field of paleobotany. Because it was printed in brown ink, the work has been described as having a "gloomy" appearance (Cave and Wakeman, 25), but in fact, the delicacy of many plates (see page 108) demonstrate not only Auer's mastery of the process but also the ability of nature printing to achieve a kind of detail unknown in any other type of botanical illustration.[16]

The same may be said of Henry Bradbury's illustrations for *Ferns of Great Britain and Ireland*, with text by the botanist Thomas Moore. It was published in parts between 1855 and 1857 in the same oversized format, but with fern specimens printed in color—shades of green and brown. Bradbury described his painstaking method for applying different colored inks to the plate before printing it in one pass through the press:

[16] In 1748, Johann Michael Seligmann, an engraver from Nuremberg, produced a volume of nature-printed skeletonized leaves set in baroque cartouches: *Die Nahrungs-Gefaesse in den Blattern* (see page 103). The delicacy of the prints, which crisply reproduce the detailed leaf venation, suggests that Seligmann must have used some type of printing plate to achieve this result, more than a hundred years before the experiments of Auer, Bradbury, and others.

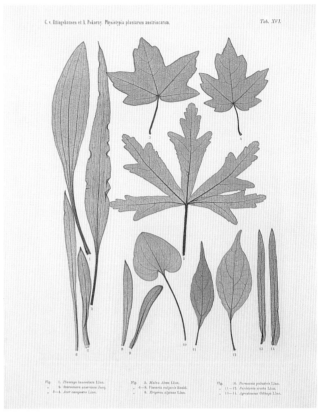

Electrotype nature prints. Skeletonized leaves. *Ettingshausen and Pokorny, Physiotypa Plantarum Austriacarum,* 1855. Printed by Alois Auer. 14 x 10¼ in.

In such cases where there are three, four, or more colours, for instance—as in flowering plants, having stems, roots, leaves, and flowers—the plan adopted in the inking of the plate is to apply the darkest colour first, which generally happens to be the roots—the superfluous colour is cleaned off—the next darkest colour, such as perhaps the colour of the stems, is then applied—the superfluous colour of which is also cleaned off—this mode is continued until every part of the plant has received its right colour. In this state, before the plate is printed, the colours in the different parts of the copper look as if the plant was imbedded in the copper. By putting in the darkest colour at the beginning, there is less chance of smearing the lighter ones: the printer too is not only able by this means to blend one colour into another, but to print all the colours at one single impression.

Bradbury's work received high praise in the January 1857 issue of London's *Quarterly Review.* This particular issue was concerned entirely with ferns—re-

viewing seven new books on the subject. The fern, which was the plant-of-the-moment in Victorian England, had provoked an indoor gardening craze (see page 37), but it also inspired serious botanical treatises. The *Review* credited the plant, only partially correctly, with having given rise to "the new art of nature-printing." In this last regard, the publication singled out "the beautiful work of [Henry] Bradbury." Here were botanical illustrations remarkable not only for the realistic delineation of the forms of the plants but, as the *Review* noted, for "the delicate veining of the foliage and the fruit-heaps [spores] on the fertile leaves [which] are brought clearly out [and appear] more distinctly than in the real objects, and in this respect are an assistance to the botanist in deciphering, as it were, the fern itself." Bradbury's accomplishment was indeed a milestone in printed illustration.

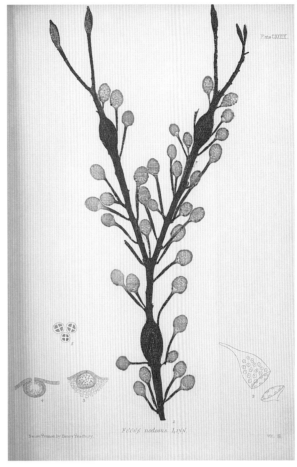

Title page from *British Sea Weeds*, 1859, with an electrotype nature-printed illustration by Henry Bradbury from the book. Collection of Philip Taaffe.

In the preface to *Ferns of Great Britain and Ireland*, the editor of the book, John Lindley, makes a point that the work "owes its origin" to "the process of the Imperial Printing Office at Vienna," although Auer is not specifically mentioned. Lindley also goes into great detail in his explanation of the benefits of nature printing to the study of botany.

He points out that art can never hope to faithfully reproduce the "minute peculiarities" of plants, especially the complex forms of ferns, "which baffle the most skilful [*sic*] and patient artist." Not until "nature-printing was brought to its present state of perfection," he says, was this accomplished.

Lindley maintains that even earlier, cruder examples of nature printing produced better results than an artist could achieve. "No one who had ever seen a Rose-leaf," he says, "could fail to recognise its impression." He admits that nature printing can show only what "lies upon the surface, and not the whole even of that. But on the other hand," he says, "its accuracy is perfect as far as it goes."

In 1859, Bradbury produced plates for a four-volume work, *Nature-Printed British Seaweeds*, by W. Johnstone and A. Croall. The result (see above) was an uncommonly beautiful botanical text in a smaller format with nature prints of unsurpassed delicacy. More books were planned, on mosses, ferns, lichens, and trees, but on September 1, 1860, Henry Bradbury committed suicide by drinking prussic acid, a seemingly senseless death that has never been explained.

Plate XLIV.

NATURE PRINTING. Pteris aquilina

PRINTED BY BRADBURY & EVANS, WHITEFRIARS, LONDON.

above and opposite: Pages from the 1855 *Ferns of Great Britain and Ireland*, with Henry Bradbury's electrotype print of *Pteris acquilina*, above, and *Atheyrium filix-foemina*, opposite. Each 21³/₄ x 14½ in.

Plate XXX.

NATURE PRINTING.

Athyrium Filix-fœmina.

PRINTED BY BRADBURY & EVANS, WHITEFRIARS, LONDON.

12

L. Dalbergia
N. name Sissoo or Sheshum

June 10ᵗʰ 72

"Dawal"
10 miles from Murree
Aug.ᵗ 30ᵗʰ 1872

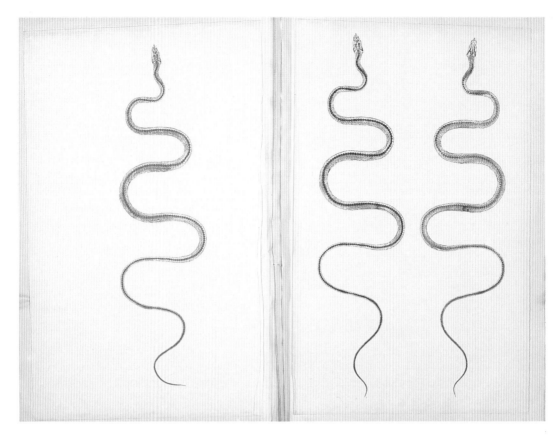

A rare, oversized nature-printed album of exotica flora and fauna produced in 1857 by Henry Smith, director of the Government Press in Madras, India. The snake print, above, which shows both back and front, was made by inking both sides of the reptile and printing it within a folded sheet of paper. Double page: 11 x 22 in. New York Botanical Garden.

In the same year, Auer received a blow when a new finance minister decided to eliminate the *Naturselbstdruck* program at the Printing Office. He was able to produce five more volumes of the *Physiotypia*, but he died in 1869, before their publication in 1873.

With the deaths of Auer and Bradbury, the commercial nature-printing process they developed ceased to exist. No doubt the electrotype technology proved too costly and complex, especially as it depended upon the incorporation of real plants. At the same time, the nascent art of photography offered a revolutionary approach to book illustration. However, nature printing—in its original, simple, direct-print method—continued to be used throughout the century by botanists in the field, recording the flora of exotic regions. One such album, *Specimens of Nature Printing from Unprepared Plants*, was produced by Henry Smith, superintendent of the Government Press in Madras in 1857, and included not only plants but also examples of animal and insect life (see above). In the 1860s, James Sinclair, with his wife, Ellen, produced several portfolios of fern and gum-leaf prints that probably recorded the flora of Melbourne, Australia, where he worked as a designer and landscaper (Hochberg, 10).[17] Also in Australia around the turn of the century, Harry Deane, a well-known amateur paleobotanist, pro-

---

[17] The Sinclair prints are housed in the National Herbarium Library of Melbourne, Australia.

Additional pages from the nature-printed album of exotica flora and fauna produced in 1857 by Henry Smith, director of the Government Press in Madras, India. Double page: 11 x 22 in. New York Botanical Garden.

duced a large number of leaf prints that recorded the venation in both living and fossil plants (Hochberg, 14).

By the early twentieth century, botanical nature printing had fallen into decline.[18] Interest was revived again in America in the mid-1970s with the establishment of the Nature Printing Society by a group of artists and hobbyists who desired to share information and ideas (see Appendix C, page 150). Now thriving, with several hundred members, the society was modeled on a Japanese association of fish printers called *Gyotaku no-kai*, whose charming and curious art had been practiced since the nineteenth century.

Collectors who today are discovering the striking beauty of old nature prints invariably share the view of a writer in the *London Review* of 1857 who described Henry Bradbury's magnificent achievement. A method had been found, he wrote, "to make Nature herself paint her own portraits with the most scrupulous fidelity."

pages 112–113 and overleaf: Nature prints of dalbergia, dawal, and lotus plants from a herbarium made in Kashmir, 1872. All 17¾ x 10¾ in.

---

[18] However, nature-printing methods were appropriated by the science of criminology for fingerprinting, which became part of standard police procedure, and also by the veterinary field, which used noseprinting of livestock to aid in tracking lost or stolen animals.

L. Nelumbium Speciosus

The Lotus
Manus Bhul Lake
Cashmere
Sepr 16t 72

The Lotus
Manus Bhul Lake. Cashmere
Sep: 16th 72.

sun
pictures

"The Glorious Sun stays in his course

& plays the Alchemyst."

—*William Shakespeare, from* King John

Photogram collage with Shakespearean quotation.
Mid-nineteenth century. 9¾ x 11 in. Courtesy
of Hans P. Kraus, Jr., New York.

BY THE MID-1800S, around the time that Auer and Bradbury were feuding over nature-printing patents, a miraculous new invention—photography—had gripped the imagination of the civilized world. The implications of photography were enormous and far-reaching. It would revolutionize book illustration; it would provide an "instant" method for recording every aspect of human life and natural phenomena; and, like nature printing, it would allow anyone to become an artist of sorts.

Where direct nature printing was a simple mechanical process (ink a leaf and print it), photography seemed magical: a picture virtually "drew itself" through the interaction of light and chemistry. Sun pictures, also called photograms or direct sun prints, were among the earliest kinds of photographs. They were lenseless and cameraless, made by placing an object, such as a plant or feather or bit of lace, directly on photosensitive paper. A piece of glass was placed over both paper and object and all were then set together in the sun. Areas of the paper exposed to the light would darken, leaving a same-size negative image where the object had been. These were the first successful photographic paper prints.

In the 1830s, the English scientist William Henry Fox Talbot, who is considered the inventor of modern photography, made extraordinary sun pictures that were soft-edged, impressionistic, and sometimes delicately colored in shades of lavender, sepia,

Photogram. Albumen print from an album of botanical photograms, mid-nineteenth century. Courtesy of Simon Lowinsky Gallery and Solomon Fine Art.

rose, and chartreuse.[19] Talbot described this visual quality as "Rembrandtish" (Rosenblum 1984, 29) and called this new art *sciagraphy,* the depiction of shadows (Schaaf, 1985, 7). He also produced images in small boxlike "cameras" fitted inside with photosensitive paper. Talbot aimed his camera at a subject—a tree or building—and reflected light would strike the paper and form an image. He called these pictures photogenic drawings, by which he meant pictures that drew themselves. In a letter explaining the process, he commented on a photogenic drawing he had made of a house: "And this I believe to be the first instance on record, of a house having painted its own portrait" (Smith 1990, 18).

Talbot had a brilliant mind and diverse interests that included astronomy, mathematics, the study of cuneiform hieroglyphics, and gardening. He was an avid horticulturalist and corresponded with several of his friends, two botanists among them, about plants. To one, Antonio Bertolini, he wrote of his belief that photography—especially when harnessed to microscopy (photos taken through a microscope)—would have great usefulness to botanists, enabling them to make instant visual records of plants "with a great deal of ease" (Buckland 1980, 19).

In 1839, the year Talbot had made public announcement of his invention, a London businessman, Rudolph Ackermann, advertised for sale "photogenic drawing box[es] with brushes, [and] chemicals...for making sun pictures...recommended for Botanists, Entymologists, and the Scientific...sufficiently clear to enable ladies to practice this pleasing art" (Ewing 1991, 15).

Women did indeed participate in the new photography, notably Talbot's wife, Constance (considered the first woman photographer), who assisted him by mixing and applying chemicals to the papers on which the pictures would print. Another woman, Anna Atkins, produced the first botanical work—on seaweeds—illustrated entirely with photographs. Atkins was a contemporary of Talbot and undoubtedly had seen examples of photograms that he had sent to her father, George Children, a noted scientist and a fellow and secretary of the Royal Society. Through her father, Atkins had come to know many eminent scientists, among them the astronomer Sir John Herschel, who had provided Talbot with critical help in perfecting the photographic process. Herschel had also coined the word photography, literally "light writing," for the new technology and the terms "negative" and "positive" for the two photographic stages as we know them today (Rosenblum, 27).

Herschel had also invented a variant of the sun print called the cyanotype, which is known familiarly today as the blueprint. The chemicals used to coat cyanotype paper were not silver based, making the process fairly easy—and also economical—to use.

Anna Atkins adopted the cyanotype as the medium for her botanical work. It was a felicitous choice

---

[19] The chemical formulas used in early photography often varied as inventors like Talbot continued to experiment. Often, beautiful color variations resulted.

the pencil of nature

William Henry Fox Talbot. Photogenic drawing negative of a Buckler fern, 1839 or earlier. 5½ x 7½ in. Courtesy of Hans P. Kraus, Jr., New York.

Between June 1844 and April 1845, Fox Talbot published a thoroughly unique book, *The Pencil of Nature*, which was his "declaration of paper photography as a vital new medium" (Buckland, 78). It was intended to publicize his invention of the reproducible image and was published in parts, each of which contained a descriptive text and examples of sun prints and photogenic drawings of various scenes and still lifes. As such, it became the first book ever to be illustrated with photographs and thus an instant milestone in the history of photography. Beaumont Newhall, the noted American historian of photography believed that its importance in the field of photography was "comparable to that of the Gutenberg Bible in printing" (Buckland, 83).

To create the plates for *The Pencil of Nature*, Talbot established a workshop at Reading, which was halfway between his home, Lacock Abbey, and London. The Reading Establishment, as it was called, functioned much as a contemporary photo shop, developing prints from negatives, albeit laying them out on racks in direct sunlight to do so.

The sun pictures produced for *The Pencil of Nature* included both photograms (camerless images) and photogenic drawings (made with the a primitive box camera and focusing lens). The former were largely pictures of leaves, lace, and feathers; the latter were scenes, made both indoors and out in a variety of picturesque locations. Exterior views included many genre scenes taken on the grounds of Lacock Abbey—carts and ladders, for example, and the stable court—while interior pictures were atmospheric still lifes of books on bookshelves, collections of glassware and china, and a classical bust taken from different angles. In every case, Talbot demonstrated the then amazing ability of photography to record detail and varying textures. Placing these images in a book set them apart from the daguerreotype and heralded the advent of the photographically illustrated book.

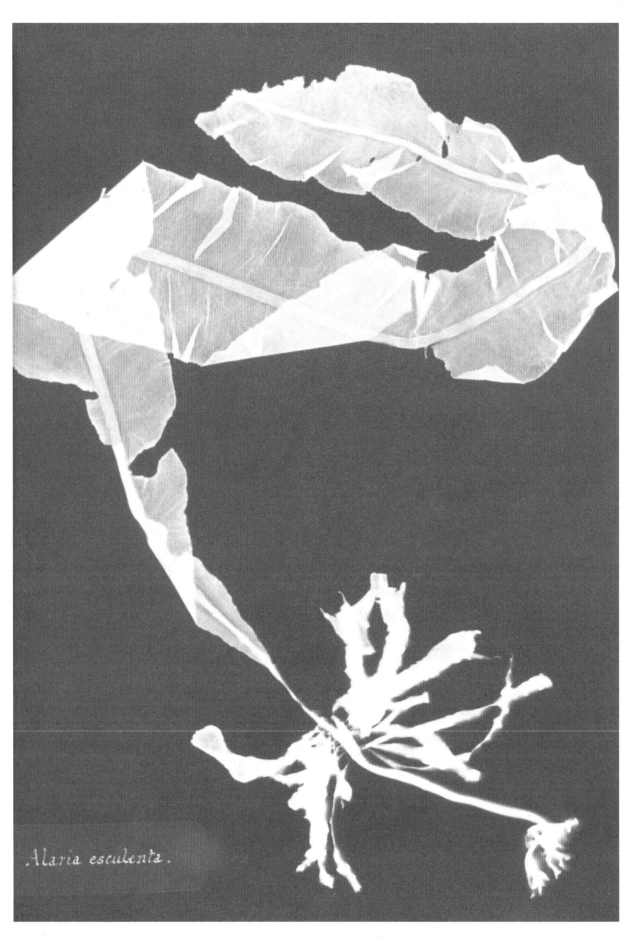

Alaria esculenta.

above and opposite: Anna Atkins. Cyanotypes from *British Algae*, 1843–1853. above: *Alaria esculenta;* opposite: *Dictyota dichotoma.* Courtesy of the Spencer Collection, New York Public Library: Astor, Lenox and Tilden Foundation.

Dictyota dichotoma
in the young state, &
in fruit.

as the watery blue background proved to be entirely appropriate for her "flowers of the sea,"[20] which seem to float in their natural element. Translucent plants appear—to modern eyes—like X-ray photos in which there is an illusory effect of depth and movement.

Like the photogram, the cyanotype had drawbacks for botanical purposes in that the opaque parts of plants appeared as negative white space—hardly detailed enough for serious study. But Anna Atkins, an accomplished watercolor artist and draftsman, with, as her father said, "a great fondness for botany" (Schaaf, 40), used the process impressively. She made a painstaking record of thousands of examples of British algae (seaweeds) and other plants over a ten-year period. Her important botanical work, *British Algae,* was the first significant departure from herbaria illustrated with real plant specimens, nature prints, or drawings.

British Algae was executed between 1843 and 1853 at the height of the natural history craze that swept England. It was a daunting, labor-intensive task. First, a paper had to be prepared for each plant by applying the appropriate chemicals using a sponge or brush. (After printing, the image was fixed by rinsing it thoroughly in water.) Next, the various species of seaweed had to be collected at the seaside, cleaned, dried, pressed, and labeled.[21] For Atkins, the process was compounded by her need to make many copies of one specimen in order to make "editions" of her book. This necessitated lifting a plant specimen from one prepared sheet of paper to another, repeating the sun exposure each time, each plant, resulting in hundreds of exposures. In addition, the plates had to be identified with the botanical name of the specimen, a task Anna accomplished with handwritten labels that she pasted on the cyanotype paper beneath each plant before printing.

In the summer of 1852, her father died and Anna was plunged into grief. She was comforted by a friend, Anne Dixon, who came to visit, then became deeply involved in the algae project. She is believed to have contributed several outstanding cyanotypes to Anna's volumes before going on to produce her own book, *Cyanotypes of British and Foreign Ferns* in 1853.

Anna Atkins presented several museums and botanical libraries in England and Scotland with complete sets—more than three hundred plates in each—of *British Algae.* Her work is treasured today mainly for its innovative and artistic use of the cyanotype process, what has been called "powerful early examples of the expressive potential of photography" (Schaaf, 40).

opposite: Photogram. Albumen print from an album of botanical photograms, mid-nineteenth century. Courtesy of Simon Lowinsky Gallery and Solomon Fine Art.

---

[20] A contemporary poem read: "Call us not weeds,—we are flowers of the sea,/For lovely and bright and gay-tinted are we;/And quite independent of culture or shower,/Then call us not weeds,—we are ocean's gay flowers."

[21] For an indication of the difficulty of collecting, see the excerpt from a Victorian guide to "Sea Mosses" in Appendix B, page 141.)

Beyond Sun Pictures

Although the photogram technique would continue to interest Victorian botanists[22] and art photographers—Julia Margaret Cameron was one—it was superseded by Talbot's invention of the calotype process, the true antecedent of modern photography. The calotype produced a latent or invisible image from which paper contact prints could be made. At the time that Anna Atkins and others were exploring the limits of sun pictures, photography employing well-crafted cameras and focusing lenses was evolving into a sophisticated new art form. The dageurreotype, invented in 1839, was enjoying immense popularity—particularly as a portrait medium—in Europe and America. At the same time, Fox Talbot and others continued to perfect new methods of making photographic prints from negatives. By midcentury, photographers were producing prints of astonishing beauty and clarity, far removed from Talbot's first grainy images. Many chose their subjects from nature, with flowers a distinct favorite. Artfully composed photographs modeled on the seventeenth-century Dutch and Flemish "flower piece" became the specialty of several French photographers such as Hippolyte Bayard and Eugene Chauvigne. Hand-

opposite and left: Bertha E. Jaques. Cyanotype series. left to right: *Seeds Falling, Curled Dock; More Seeds Gone, Curled Dock; More Seeds Gone, Curled Dock*, 1905–1915. Courtesy of Hans P. Kraus, Jr.

---

[22] A fascinating variant of the sun print, made with thinly sliced sections of different types of wood, was described in *The Popular Science Monthly* in 1894. Sun printing produced highly detailed images that were then used to produce the plates used in photoengraving.

Anonymous. Albumen print. left: *Nectaroscila hyacinthoides*, circa 1880s. 11 x 8½ in.; right: *Orchis ustulata*, 1870s. 10⅛ x 8½ in. Courtesy of Gary Edwards Gallery.

colored flower photographs were adopted by greeting card manufacturers, and flower photographs were used as aids in teaching fine and applied art (Ewing, 32).

Some of the earliest botanical photographs, made in the 1850s and 1860s, are cross-sections of flowers, but it was not until the early twentieth century that botanical photography began to come into its own as a scientific tool. The most stunning innovation was the radiograph, or X-ray photo, which had been invented in 1895 but was not widely used until 1912. The radiograph enabled botanists to view the interior structure of plants without having to dissect them but its beauty also enthralled numerous art photographers who have used it up to the present day.

In the early decades of the century, outstanding botanical studies of plants were made by several pho-tographers, whose work was presented in the 1991 exhibition *Flora Photographica*. They included the clergyman and mycologist E. T. Harper, the pictorial photographer Henry Troth, and Edwin Hale Lincoln, who produced the extraordinary portfolio of four hundred plants *Wildflowers of New England*. By the 1920s and 1930s, full-scale botanical texts with photographic illustrations began to appear, thus fulfilling the promise of the new medium.[23]

Although botanical photography became the primary mode for recording species, it did not eliminate the need for collecting specimens. Both are essential modes of record keeping that serve the scientist in different ways. And both have captured the imaginations of artists, for whom plant forms—endlessly varied and profoundly expressive—remain objects of beauty and mystery.

---

[23] Examples of these and other works mentioned in this paragraph are reproduced in *Flora Photographica*.

Edwin Hale Lincoln. *Asclepias tuberosa.* Orange milkweed. Platinum print, circa 1905. 9¼ x 7¼ in.

afterword:
the persistence of botany: real plants in contemporary art

The real plant as visual metaphor figures importantly in the work of several leading twenthieth-century artists, each of whom has made a unique appropriation of either the botanical specimen, the nature print, or the photogram. In the hands of these artists, the plant becomes a resonant symbol, an image evocative of myth, literature, and the eternal cycles of life, death, and rebirth.

Two who have used botanical materials, and even living plants, to powerful effect are the post-modernist German artists Joseph Beuys (d. 1986) and Anselm Kiefer (b. 1945), who was Bueys's student and disciple. Both rejected the modernist dictum that "the only subject for art is art" and turned instead to ecological issues and postwar Germany's moral and physical devastation as content for their work.

Beuys took as one of his central themes the need to reconnect nature and culture, an idea that he often expressed through drawings, but also through shamanistic and ecology-based "actions." His most significant art action was *Seven Thousand Oaks*, a 1982 Documenta 7 project, which required as many trees to be planted in German cities in a gesture of "afforestation as redemption" (Schama, 124).

In 1985, Beuys adopted the concept of the herbarium—a systematic collection of pressed and dried plants—to create a series of fourteen drawings that he called *Ombelico de Venere-Cotyledon Umbilicus Veneris.* The title's reference is to the umbilical cord of Venus with its connotations of birth, sex, and fertility; but Beuys's choice of the pressed plant may also be read variously as a metaphor for death and eternity, or an ecological plea for preservation of nature, or even possibly a reference to alchemy—as the plant turns golden with age. The herbarium concept reflects as well Beuys's life-long interest in natural history and classification, and is manifest in several drawings that he conceived as written lists. An early example of this is Herb Robert (1941), a handwritten list on paper of healing, oil-bearing plants with two pressed plants at the center. Such a literal connection between art and nature was often at the core of Beuys's work, which sometimes utilized plant juices as pigment, and in one instance, *Monument to the Stag* (1958), to the use of rubbed moss as a coloring agent.

Anselm Kiefer's immense, theatrically constructed and visually complex art works share Beuys's connection to the earth, but even more specifically to Germany's earth and forests, to its myth and literature, especially as it pertains to regeneration in the post-Nazi era. In Kiefer's monumental landscapes, figures or names from German myth and history overlay images of scorched-earth or bloodied, ruined forests. In many such paintings, Keifer uses a variety of unorthodox and metaphorically charged materials,

opposite: Alselm Keifer. *Horus.* Lead, steel, and dried sunflowers, 1998. Photo by Margrit Olsen. Courtesy of Gagosian Gallery.

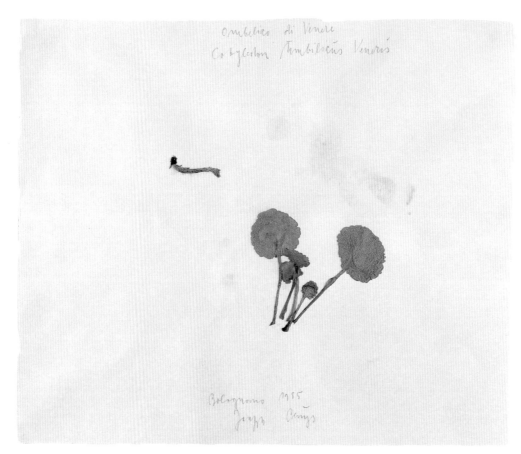

Joseph Beuys. *Ombelico de Venere-Cotyledon Umbilicus Veneris.*
Pressed plant on paper; inscribed in pencil, 1985. Courtesy of Heiner Bastian Gallery.

such as lead, straw, and pressed ferns, to create heavily worked surfaces that refer to cultural archetypes, and in later works, to cosmic or primordial space.

For Kiefer the fern represents geologic time; it is one of the most ancient plants, those which have decomposed over eons to form the coal deposits that made Germany the premier coal-mining region in Europe. Hence, the fern symbolizes for him an energy source; but it also has archaic associations drawn from early German culture, specifically the custom of gathering fern seeds at the summer solstice that were to be used in mysterious rituals (Rosenthal, M. 1987, 153).

In his 1998 sculpture *Horus* (see page 130), named for the Egyptian sun god, Kiefer uses a favorite image, the lead book, to create a ponderous mythic herbarium, in which dried sunflowers erupt from the weighty pages as if thrust from the history of a ravaged earth.

Apart from its geologic and mythic associations, the fern is also appreciated by artists for its flat, graphic structure and dramatic form. As we have seen in the previous chapter, the nineteenth-century nature printer Henry Bradbury developed a new technology for reproducing images of ferns and algae, and it is these very nature-printed images that have attracted the American artist Philip Taaffe, who is known for graphically complex and densely patterned paintings and drawings. Taaffe is a collector of nineteenth- and twentieth-century illustrated books on natural history, from which he has been building "a vocabulary of images" that he uses in his work. "I'm always looking for something so representative of its type that it almost becomes an abstract element," says Taaffe, "a distillation or encapsulation of its varieties" (*Composite Nature* 1997, 5). Responding to the raw graphic power of the nineteenth-century images—ferns, shells, and sea creatures—Taaffe photographs them and incorporates them, along with his own drawings, into layered, dynamic compositions, which convey the illusion of remarkable depth despite the flatness of surface. Like Andy Warhol, Taaffe uses a silk-screen process to make repeat images, but the resultant work could not be more dissimilar. Warhol's flat, Pop-art portraits and flower prints celebrate the superficial surface, while Taaffe's iconic "drawings," rendered with luminous oil-based pigment, convey a sense of place in nature, be it forest or sea. "I want the viewer to come away with a very detailed memory of having been there," he says, "having seen this thing, having experienced what I experienced, in the making of it" (*Composite Nature*, 110).

Adam Fuss. *Untitled.* Cibachrome photogram, 1993.
14 x 11 in. Courtesy of Cheim & Read Gallery.

Visual immediacy is also a primary quality in the photograms of Adam Fuss. Photograms are normally made as contact prints, by pressing plants or other flat objects to sensitized paper and exposing it to light. Fuss uses the same basic principle but deliberately subverts the process by placing cibachrome film under a transparent glass tray of water. The subject to be photographed floats in the water, which acts as a

sort of amniotic lens, bending the light from above so that plants and other objects print on the cibachrome in unearthly auras and in varying stages of focus. As in Fox Talbot's earliest attempts at photography, an ineffable image results through the interaction of light and chemistry; but by introducing water and cibachrome to the equation, Fuss embues the photogram with qualities of depth and color that Fox Talbot may have dreamed of, but that Anna Atkins could not have imagined as she "floated out" her seaweeds to be pressed and printed by the cyanotype method in the 1830s.

For these and other contemporary artists who use botanical materials, the plant provides a tangible link between art and nature. Its presence in a work of art is a demonstration of form and beauty that no illustration can rival; and, at the same time, it provides an opportunity to discover both art and nature anew. What we see, and what we hope this book reveals, is that the plant itself remains the most provocative of symbols, a talisman of this earth's eternal truths, beauties, and mysteries.

overleaf: Philip Taaffe. *Adiantum.* Oil pigment on canvas, 1997. 63⅞ x 55 in. Photo by Steven Sloman. Courtesy of the artist.

appendix a:
collecting and preserving plant specimens

There are many reasons and ways to collect plant specimens. You may wish to create an ongoing herbarium record of your garden, including examples of new plants added each year. Or, inspired by examples shown in Part One of this book, you may want to create framed specimens for your home, or use pressed plants as inclusions in travel diaries. The guidelines in this section are designed to help you collect, preserve, and mount specimens according to professional botanical practice, with the result that your work will last for years to come.

Where to Collect The best place to start collecting plant specimens is in your own backyard or, with permission, in the backyards of friends and neighbors. Do not collect on private or public lands without permission. The National Park Service, which oversees all national parks in the United States, allows a person to take specimens from a park only if he or she is conducting research and only with written permission obtained beforehand. State and local

Ellen Quillin, a noted Texas botanist, is shown with her collecting case, called a vasculum, in a photograph from the 1920s. San Antonio Light Collection. Courtesy of Institute of Texan Cultures, San Antonio, Texas.

parks may have more liberal regulations, but always ask for permission before you take a specimen. For information about where to apply for permits, contact:

> Luis A. Ruedas
> Museum of Southwestern Biology
> University of New Mexico
> Albuquerque, New Mexico 87131-1091
> Phone: (505) 277-5340
> Fax: (505) 277-3838
> E-mail at: lruedas@sevilleta.unm.edu
> or you can visit his Web site at: *http://sevilleta.unm.edu/~lruedas/permits.html*

Native Plant Societies Most states have native plant societies that can connect you with an informal network of amateur plant collectors. Through the societies, one can meet a range of plant enthusiasts, from professional botanists to groups of hikers interested in learning about local flora. The California Native Plant Society is particularly well-organized and has a Web site:

http://www.calpoly.edu/~dchippin/cnps main.html

Endangered Plants The aim of the Park Service is to maintain the integrity of park lands and to protect wild and endangered plant species. The following guides to endangered plants are recommended for collectors and plant enthusiasts alike:

Vanishing Flora: Endangered Plants Around the World.
Dugald Stermer. New York: Harry N. Abrams, 1995.
(191 pages. $39.95).

This book is written for a lay audience and includes eight-five beautiful graphite and watercolor renderings of plants in danger of extinction. The appendix lists conservation organizations.

Endangered and Threatened Plants of the United States.
Edward S. Ayensu. Washington: Smithsonian Institution
Press, 1978. ($46.00).

A thorough guide to endangered plants in all parts of the United States.

National Audubon Society Field Guides: *California,*
Florida, New England, The Pacific Northwest, The Mid-
Atlantic, The Southeast, The Southwest, The Rocky Mountains.
New York: The National Audubon Society. ($19.95 each).

Each pocket-sized guide of 450 pages contains more than 1,500 full-color photographs plus hundreds of color illustrations and maps. Nearly a thousand frequently encountered plants, including those that are endangered—and animals—are shown and described in detail, as are fifty of the best natural sites in each region.

Collecting Guidelines You don't need special equipment to collect and press plants. A forty-eight-page pamphlet, "Plant Collecting for the Amateur" by T. Christopher Brayshaw, describes collection procedures and techniques using mainly household items. It is available for $8.95 from The Royal British Museum Shop, Box 9815 Stn. Prov. Govt, Victoria, British Columbia, Canada V8V, 1W4, Canada; Fax:

(250) 356-8197. The following guidelines have been adapted and excerpted from that publication. Another excellent source is "Expert Secrets for Preserving Plants" by Shawn Carlson, *Scientific American*, June 1999.

Materials   Before setting out to collect, assemble the following materials:

P L A S T I C   B A G S .   Garbage bags or food-storage bags keep specimens fresh for a day or so until ready for pressing.

N E W S P A P E R .   Cut large sheets of newspaper (broadsheet-sized) down the fold, then fold again across the middle to make just the right size folders for plants, about 11 by 17 inches. (Alternatively, you can use a telephone book for large plants or a smaller paper-back book for interleaving specimens as you collect. However, the system described here gives better results.)

C A R D B O A R D   S E P A R A T O R S .   Pieces of corrugated cardboard cut the same size as the sheets of newspaper are used in between newspaper sheets. They allow air to circulate between specimens in the press and diffuse moisture.

F E L T   O R   A B S O R B E N T   P A P E R .   This accommodates thin stems while pressing the leaves flat. Cut pieces the same size as separators.

F O A M   R U B B E R .   Useful for pressing speci-mens with thick stems or fruit. Accommodates thick parts while pressing foliage flat. A variety of thicknesses is useful.

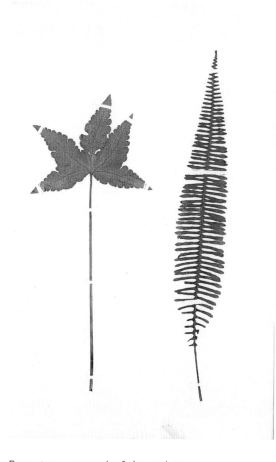

Paper tape secures leaf tips and stems.

P R E S S   B A C K S .   Used for constructing a plant press these are strips of wood lath, or two pieces of quarter-inch plywood, cut to 11 by 17 inches.

S T R A P S   O R   C O R D .   These should be strong enough to tie the press together tightly. Bungee cords can be used.

When to Collect Dry weather is best for collecting plants to press and preserve. Plants collected in wet weather take longer to dry in the press and can become moldy or discolored. In general, the faster a plant dries, the better its color is preserved.

What to Collect A scientific specimen includes every part of the plant necessary for identification. However, specimens collected for personal or decorative reasons need not be as complete. Specimens of herbaceous plants should include at least part of the stems, leaves, and flowers or fruit. In grasses, sedges, and rushes, and some other groups, it is often important to include a bit of the root system. Tree and shrub specimens should include twigs, leaves, and flowers, cones or catkins.

Take care not to mix the flowers or fruits of different plants. When your specimens are eventually mounted permanently on a sheet, the parts of only one species from one locality should appear on one sheet. Don't press bulky cones or seed pods; keep them in paper bags or envelopes numbered to correspond with the twig and foliage portions of the same specimens.

Specimens should include collecting data: location, date, collector's name, and preferably some notes on habitat. Flower color may also be included, as the color may fade in drying.

Pressing Before plant specimens can be mounted, they must first be pressed and dried. To achieve well-pressed plants, lay each specimen, as it is collected, in a folded newspaper page, arranged as it will look on the mounting sheet. Write collecting information on the margin of the newspaper or in a notebook with a number corresponding to the numbered specimen.

To Make the Press The press is made up as follows: On one press back (rigid board or plywood) lay a corrugated cardboard separator, then a specimen in its newspaper folder, a piece of felt, absorbent paper, or foam rubber; then repeat the succession, starting with another specimen, until the day's take is completed. At the end of the collecting day, place the second press back on top and secure tightly with cord. This is important to ensure that leaves are pressed flat. Open the press once a day to check specimens and remove them as they become dry.

Mounting and Filing Dried Specimens For best results in mounting dried specimens, botanists recommend using high-quality materials:

M O U N T I N G   S H E E T S . Heavy white, acid-free paper with one-hundred-percent rag content is best, but if not available, use any stiff white paper. However, over time, impurities in lesser grades of paper will damage your specimens. Purchase sheets in the standard herbarium size used in North America, about 11 by 17 inches.

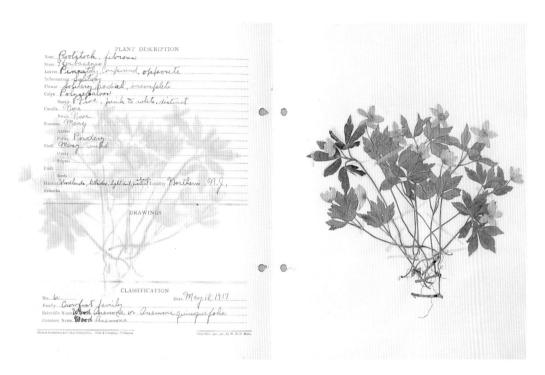

A prepeprinted, spiral-bound herbarium from 1917.

L A B E L S . These can be simple or fancy, typed or handwritten, but should be large enough to carry the collecting information you wish to include. You may even write directly on the mounting sheet; however, if you make a mistake, the sheet will be spoiled.

G U M M E D   P A P E R   O R   C L O T H   A D H E S I V E   T A P E . To fasten specimens to paper sheets, cut tape or paper into narrow strips and place across the stems and ends. Do not use Scotch tape or other plastic tapes, because they will become brittle over time.

P L A S T I C   C E M E N T . Not to be confused with rubber cement. Large herbariums often use plastic cement (such as Elmer's glue) to fasten specimens to sheets. Herbarium glue or paste, with thinner, can be purchased from a biological or scientific supply store.

NEEDLE AND THREAD. To fasten thick parts of specimens to sheets, use strong white thread (it won't discolor the specimen).

MAGNIFYING GLASS, TWEEZERS, SCALPEL OR KNIFE, SCISSORS, AND NEEDLES. All are useful in preparing and identifying specimens.

POLYETHYLENE BAGS. Plastic bags will protect specimens from physical damage and keep insects out. Polyethylene plastic does not exude chemicals harmful to specimens. The bags should be large enough to fit over a group of folders.

FILING CABINET. Store specimens in their folders, contained in plastic bags, in an insect-proof cabinet. Steel filing cabinets are ideal; but as long as specimens are enclosed in plastic bags, cardboard cartons will do.

Mounting Specimens

The traditional method that is to mount only one specimen from one location to a sheet. However, two or more small specimens may be grouped, leaving space for captions or labels.

Reserve a space in the bottom right-hand corner of the sheet for the label. Botanists customarily arrange the specimen in the remaining space with the thick parts—roots, flower head, and so on—placed near the edges of the mounting sheet. However, any artistic arrangement is acceptable as long as it shows the form of the plant to optimum advantage.

Small weights are useful for holding a specimen in place while cement is being applied. Using a squeeze bottle, touch the nozzle to the sheet beside the stem and form a drop. Draw the drop over the stem to touch the sheet on the other side of the stem. Allow several hours for the cement to set; and do not stack sheets until thoroughly dry.

Sources

For professional presses and botanists' paper folders:

BioQuip
Gardenia, CA
(310) 324-0620

Fisher Science Education
Burr Ridge, IL
(800) 955-1177

appendix b:
a nineteenth-century guide to pressing and mounting seaweeds

The following instructions are reprinted verbatim from *Sea Mosses: A Collector's Guide and an Introduction to the Study of Marine Algae*, by A. B. Hervey, A.M. Boston: S. E. Cassino, 1881. Bracketed phrases have been added.

[The basic tools you will need...] For "Floating out," your "Sea Mosses," as it is called, you should provide yourself a few simple tools and requisites. You should have a pair of pliers; a pair of scissors; a stick like a common cedar "pen stalk," with a needle driven into the end of it, or, in lack of that, any stick sharpened carefully; two or three large white dishes, like "wash bowls," botanist's "drying paper," or common blotting paper; pieces of cotton cloth, old cotton is the best; and the necessary cards or papers for mounting the plants on.

[How you will be using your tools...] You will use the pliers in handling your plants in the water. The scissors you will need for trimming off the superfluous branches of plants which are too bushy too look well, when spread upon the paper, and to cut away parasites. The needle should be driven points first, a considerable distance into the stick, so as to make it firm, and allow you to use the blunt end of it in arranging the finer details of your plant on the paper.

[There are several types of drying paper...]

For drying paper, of course, you can use common newspaper, by putting many thicknesses together....But sheets of blotting paper will be found much more satisfactory, twenty-five of them cut into quarters, would probably be all you would use, and those you could easily take with you in your trunk.

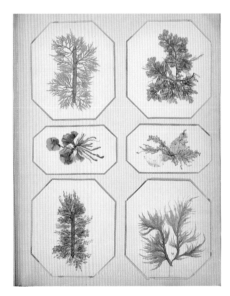

above: A rare album of sea mosses dates from the mid-nineteenth century. Artistic groupings of specimens, each set in an octagonal frame, appear as miniature paintings. Courtesy of Rick Dodge.

[Botanists' drying paper is best...] What will be found cheaper and still more servicable, if you are going to mount a large number of plants at once, is a quantity of botanist's "drying paper"... [See listing on page 152 for contemporary sources.] It is a coarse, spongy, brown felt paper, cut into sheets, 12 x 18 inches, and has a fine capacity for absorbing moisture. For convenience, the cotton cloths should be made the same size as the drying paper used.

[The best way to mount a few specimens at a time...] Some collectors, who do not care to mount a great number of specimens at once...use no drying paper at all, but in the place of it, have thin small pieces of deal [an old-fashioned term for pine board; particleboard would work as well]...a foot or so square and one-quarter or one-third of an inch thick; upon these they spread one or more layers of cotton and lay the plant on them and put as many more [layers of cotton] over it; the cotton absorbs the moisture and the boards keep the pressure even and the papers and plants straight and smooth throughout.

[There are several types of mounting paper...] For "mounting paper," each one must use his own taste. Many prefer card cut of uniform size; they can be had at almost any paper store or job printing office, made to order. Four and a half by six and a half inches is a neat and convenient size.

[An economical way to buy mounting paper...] But if you want to mount several hundred or several thousand specimens, in the course of a season, so as to have some to give to all your friends, and to make up a number of books or albums, to sell at Church or Charity fairs, then perhaps the expense will be an item worth considering. In that case you will find it cheaper to buy a few quires of good 26- or 28-lb....paper, unruled of course...in unfolded sheets, 16 x 21 inches, and will cut into convenient sizes for mounting any plant ordinarily collected. By halving it, you have sheets 8 x 21, or 10½ x 16 inches. By quartering, the sheets are 8 x 10½ inches; halving these you get an octavo sheet 5¼ x 8 inches which is quite large enough for a great majority of plants. One half of this will give a sheet 4 x 5¼ inches, which will be the size most used; while the smallest plants look best on the half of these sheets, 2½ x 4 inches.

["Floating Out" the sea mosses...]

With your large white dishes, filled near to the brim with sea-water, or, if you are away from the ocean, with water made artificially salt, take a few of your plants from the collecting case, and put them in one of the dishes. Here, handling them with your pliers, shake them out and clean them of any adhering sand or shells, trim away parasites and superfluous branches, and generally make them ready for "floating out." Thence, transfer them, one at a time, as you "float them" to the other dish.

[A little manual dexterity helps...]

Then take your card, or your paper, selecting a piece large enough to give the plant ample room, and leave a margin of white all around, and having dipped it in the water, put it quite under the floating plant, holding the paper with your left hand and managing the plant with the right. Now float the plant out over the paper, and draw the root or base of it up near to the end of the paper next your hand, so that you can hold it down on the paper with the thumb of your left hand, the rest of that hand being under the paper in the water. Now, slowly lift the paper up to the surface and draw it out of the water, in such a way that the water will flow off from it in two or three directions. This will spread the plant out somewhat evenly over the paper.

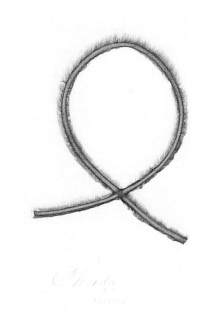

[Use the needle to arrange branches naturally...] But in many cases you will need to arrange the branches in their most natural and graceful position and also take care that they do not get massed upon each other, and make unsightly heaps, while other places are left bare. They should be carefully arranged so as to make the most beautiful picture possible. In some fine and delicate plants, too much care cannot be bestowed in having the remote branchlets all naturally disposed and spread out. This final work of arranging details, you will do with your needle while you hold the paper very near to the surface of the water with your left hand, so near, indeed, that there will be just water enough and no more, above it, to float the delicate parts which you are manipulating.

[Re-immerse plants if you need to rearrange them...] Oftentimes it will be found convenient, after the paper with plant on it has been removed from the water, to re-immerse a part of it at a time and re-arrange the several parts separately. But all this can easily be done, more easily than I can tell how to do it....A very little practice will give you the "knack" perfectly....And...if you will let them take on your paper the form and outline, which they have by nature in the water, there will be nothing left to desire, for their color, form, and movement, all combine there, to make them the loveliest and most graceful things that grow.

[Drain the arranged plants before drying...] When you have put the last finishing touches upon the "floating" process, and your "Sea Moss" is adjusted upon your paper so as to be "a thing of beauty, and a joy forever;" then...lay the paper upon some incline surface, any smooth board will do, to drain away the superfluous water. Thence it is to be transferred, in a few moments, to the press, for drying.

[Arrange the plants in the press...]

[On]...one of the above described sheets of blotting paper, botanist's "drying paper," or boards of muslin covered deal...lay your paper with the plant on it upon this, the plant up. Cover the board or drying paper all over with "float" specimens in the same way.

[Weight the boards, using care not to crush the specimens...]

Over all and lying directly upon the plants spread your piece of muslin. Upon this, put another sheet of the paper, or board, and upon this again, a layer of plants, then a piece of the muslin, more paper, plants, muslin, and so on till you have disposed of all of your collection, or so much of it as you care to mount. Upon the last layer of plants put a final sheet of paper, and over all a stout board, as large as the drying paper. Upon this lay some heavy weight.

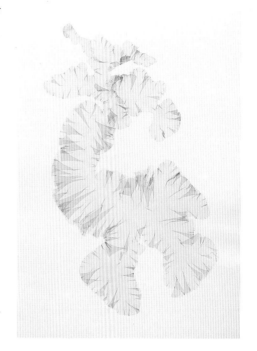

[Ideas for weighting the press...]

Stones will be as handy as anything at the sea-side...about fifty pounds of them if I were using botanist's drying paper, which has a good deal of "give" in it. With the use of boards unless there are a good many thicknesses of muslin, it would not do to weight it so heavily or some of the plants would be crushed beyond recognition. I use the drying paper, and always have two boards, one for the bottom, and one for the top of my press. Then, when I "have made the pile complete," I can put it aside in some convenient corner out of the way, and set the stones to work, bearing down on it, a business for which they seem to have some conspicuous and weighty gifts.

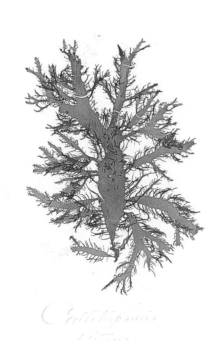

[The drying process, part one...] Some botanists recommend that the drying papers be changed in the course of five or six hours, and the cloths and papers again in twenty-four hours....But my practice [has] always been to let them lie twenty-four hours, and then give them a change of both cloths and papers, being careful in removing the cloths so as not to lift the plants from the mounting paper.

[The second drying...] The second time in the press they should be subject to a harder pressure, seventy-five or one hundred pounds of stone being not too much. In twenty-four hours more, most of them will be quite dry and ready to be put into your herbarium, album, or whatever you use for the final disposition of them. Those that are not perfectly dry should be put back in the press with dry papers and cloths for another day's stay.

[Label the specimens...] When the plant is perfectly dry, and removed from the press, you should, before putting it away and forgetting these facts, write on the back of the paper the exact date and place of collecting.

[Plants stick to the paper without glue...] People often ask me what I use to make the plants stick so firmly to the paper, supposing evidently, that it is necessary to have some kind of gum or mucilage for that purpose....I use nothing whatever...there is sufficient gelatinous matter in the body of the plant to make it perfectly adhere to the paper without other aid...the reason for putting the muslin over the plants, in the process of pressing and drying, is that they may not stick to the drying paper, which is laid above them.

[...but there are exceptions...] But a considerable number of the "Sea Mosses" do not adhere to paper well. They either have not gelatinous matter enough in them, or will not give it out to glue their bodies to the paper....In these cases...after being dried in the press in the usual way [the plant] is simply strapped down with slips of gummed paper.

[Using adhesive, tape, or even milk...]

Sometimes they are fastened down with some kind of adhesive substance, after being dried [plastic glue]...is best for this. Others tape them and float them out a second time in skimmed milk, and after wiping off the milk from the paper and plants except directly under the plants, put them in the press to dry again, when, it is said, they stay.

[Use different methods for rockweed and kelp...]

In preparing the coarser "Rockweed" and "Kelp" for the herbarium, another method will have to be pursued. These will almost all turn very dark, or quite black, in the process of drying....I spread them out in some shaded place, and let them lie for a few hours, perhaps twenty-four, perhaps less or more, until most of the water in them has evaporated, but not till they have become hard, stiff, and brittle. Then I put them between sheets of drying paper and lay them in the press, and keep them there until the process of drying is complete. A little practice will be the only way by which you will learn how to tell if they have been dried long enough in the open air. If you find them inclined to mould while kept in the press, you may be sure they are not dry enough; throw them away and get some new ones.

[Keeping specimens unmounted until ready for use...]

It is sometimes desirable to keep the treasure we have gathered from the sea unmounted, that we may carry them away to await a more convenient season for floating them out, or that we may send them to some friend or correspondent on the other side of the continent or beyond the seas...All but the more delicate and perishable of these plants may be dried rough; rolled up, and kept any length of time; transported round the world; and then, when put in water again, will come out in half an hour, as fresh and bright and supple and graceful as they were, when taken from their briny home.

[How to treat delicate plants...] Delicate... plants may be...treated...by first shaking the water out of them and then thoroughly mingling them with dry sea sand, and drying them rough in the usual way...Sand will adhere to the most delicate fibers and ramuli of the plant, in such a way as to keep them separate and present their getting glued together. Then, when they are afterwards soaked out, the sand will be disengaged and the plant left as good as ever it was.

[Soak out plants with salt water...] "Soaking out" should always be done with salt water unless you know you have only those plants that fresh water will not hurt. When I have had specimens of the "Rockweed" or "Kelp" sent me "rough dried," I have found it best to prepare them for mounting, not immersing them in water, and so getting a great quantity of moisture into them, which would have to be expelled afterwards with no little trouble, but by wrapping them about with wet towels; from these they would imbibe enough dampness to be manageable, but not enough to make them troublesome.

[How to display your plants...] Before taking leave of this part of my subject, I must...add a word in regard to a point which botanists commonly think too little about, viz: the display of taste in the mounting of their plants. To the mere botanist, a plant is a *specimen*, of a given genus and species interesting wholly for that fact....Now all are not botanists. Most of those who will read these pages will have an interest in these plants, to which the scientific interest will be secondary. I want to say then to them: look for the best things, get the whole plant when you can, but get and preserve the most perfect and beautiful plants.

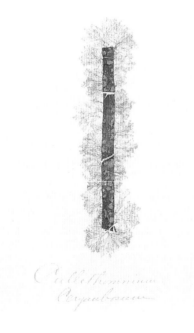

[Grouping sea mosses for best effect...] It is the rule with the botanist to put but one species on each paper or card; I certainly advise disregarding this rule, unless you are mounting for scientific purposes all together or cheaply. With the numberless shades of red which one group of "Sea Mosses" will give you, with the various kinds of green which the other two will present, you will have opportunity to display all the taste and skill you are master of. For in combining several different colors and forms, on the same paper you may often produce the most brilliant result.

[Work out lovely designs...] A little practice will soon make you able to handle two or three plants at the same time in "floating them out," almost as readily as you manage one. Then again, you will soon find it possible with some of the more slender plants to work out interesting and beautiful "designs" in the same way. Initial letters, even monograms, may not be beyond your reach with a little care and practice. Let the "Sea Mosses" contribute to the cultivation of every faculty, and all possible means of pleasure for you.

[Preserve treasures after mounting...] For preserving your treasures after they are neatly mounted, pressed and dried, you have two courses open to you. You can take care of them as a botanist does, by arranging them systematically in a herbarium, with covers of stout manilla paper folded 10½ x 16½ inches, for each genus, and the species separated by white sheets or thinner covers; or, you can provide yourself with blank books, made for the purpose, having the leaves cut to fit the sizes of paper or card which you mount your plants on, so as to slip the corners of the card into the cuts. It is well in that case to provide a book with leaves large enough to hold two or four cards each.

By following the direction here given, I cannot doubt you will soon become a successful collector, and an expert in mounting and preserving "Sea Mosses."

appendix c:
nature-printing guidelines and materials sources

The Nature Printing Society is an international organization of artists and enthusiasts of nature printing. Members receive a quarterly newsletter that includes articles on the techniques and history of nature printing. For information regarding membership contact:

> The Nature Printing Society
> Santa Barbara Museum of Natural History
> 2559 Puesta del Sol Road
> Santa Barbara, CA 93105
> Phone: (805) 682-4711, ext. 4711

The Art of Printing from Nature: A Guidebook by The Nature Printing Society is a sixty-page paperbound, illustrated manual that describes several types of nature-printing techniques, from the direct method (see below), to printing on cloth, cyanotype prints, *gyotaku* (fish printing), *takuga* (plant rubbings) and related information on materials and mounting. It is available for $9 from: Sonja Larsen, 7675 Interlachen Road, Lake Shore, MN 56468–8650.

The Direct Printing Method   When you apply ink directly to the object, such as a leaf or plant, then press it to paper, this is the direct method. Single leaves are the easiest subjects to handle and make good project for beginners. You can use fresh leaves, but pressed, dried leaves give the best result, as they lie flatter on the paper. After assembling your materials, make practice prints on newsprint until your have perfected your technique. Then proceed to fine and unusual papers. Use an ordinary stamp pad to make your first prints. Place a leaf, vein side down, on the pad with tweezers, press it down with a small square of paper to thoroughly coat it with ink. Remove paper and lift the leaf with tweezers to a clean piece of paper. Cover again with clean paper and press down gently with the heel of your hand to make the print. You can then proceed to using printing tools and materials that will give your images greater graphic scope and clarity.

Tools and Materials   A piece of glass or plastic, about 8 by 10 inches or larger is ideal. But you can use a smooth surface covered with freezer paper, taped in place.

BRAYERS. One or two brayers, which are hand-tools for rolling ink, made of soft or hard rubber. They come in various sizes, from 1- to 6-inches wide. Available in art supply stores (see page 152).

NEWSPAPER. Newsprint makes perfect practice paper. Cut large sheets of newspaper down the fold.

INK. Water-based printer's ink, of the type suitable for block printing.

OTHER TOOLS. Tweezers, palette knife, old rags, paper towels, soap and water.

Method There are several methods of inking and printing specimens. Two excellent guides that describe and illustrate a variety of approaches are the Nature Printing Society's publication, cited above, and Laura Donnelly Bethmann's *Nature Printing with Herbs, Fruits & Flowers* (see Bibliography, pages 156–157), which explains, among many other techniques, how to create a "walking press," in which the printer uses body weight to print an image.

The general approach is as follows: Assemble your materials, together with leaves and plants, in the order in which you will use them. First, scoop out a glob of ink with the palette knife and spread it onto the glass. Use the brayer to smear the ink evenly, and thinly over the glass. With a tweezer, place the object on the inked surface. At this point you can proceed in several ways. Here are two possibilities:

(a) Use a small, inked brayer to roll and press the leaf into the ink, simultaneously coating both sides. With tweezers, lift the inked leaf to one side of a sheet of newspaper, fold the sheet in half over the leaf, and, holding the stem with one hand, gently press with the other hand. When you separate the halves of the paper, you will have two images: the top and underside of the leaf. Practice your technique in this way before proceeding to the use of fine papers.

(b) After laying the specimen on the inked surface, place a piece of waxed paper over it and press gently with your hand or roll it with a brayer until it is evenly coated with ink. Remove the waxed paper and, using a tweezer, transfer the specimen to a piece of paper, inked side down. Cover with another piece of clean paper, and press with your hand or with the brayer. Remove the top paper and lift the specimen from the sheet. Allow the nature print to dry before handling.

sources for nature-printing supplies

General art supply catalogs:

ARTISTS' CONNECTION
600 U.S. Highway One S.
Iselin, NJ 08830-2635
(800) 851-9333

CHEAP JOE'S
374 Industrial Park Rd.
Boone, NC 28607
(800) 227-2788

DANIEL SMITH
4150 First Ave. S.
Box 84268
Seattle, WA 98124-5568
(800) 426-6740

DICK BLICK ART
Box 1267
Galesburg, IL 61402-1267
(800) 828-4548

OTT'S DISCOUNT
ART SUPPLY
102 Hungate Dr.
Greenville, NC 27858
(800) 356-3289

SAX ARTS & CRAFTS
Box 51710
New Berlin, WI 53151
(800) 323-0388

TRIARCO ARTS
& CRAFTS, INC.
14650 28th Ave. N.
Plymouth, MN 55447
(800) 328-3360
In MN: (800) 635-9361

UNITED ART &
EDUCATION SUPPLY
Box 9219
Fort Wayne, IN 46899
(800) 322-3247

Papers and art supplies:

A & B SMITH
Box 1776
Pittsburgh, PA 15230-1776
(412) 242-5400

AIKO'S ART MATERIALS
3347 N. Clark St.
Chicago, IL 60657
(773) 404-5600

CHINA CULTURAL
CENTER
210 Mandarin Place
970 N. Broadway
Los Angeles, CA 90012
(213) 489-3827

DOLPHIN PAPERS
1125 Brookside Ave. G900
Indianapolis, IN 46202
(800) 346-2770

NEW YORK CENTRAL
SUPPLY CO.
62 Third Ave.
New York, NY 10003
(212) 477-0400

ORIENTAL ART SUPPLY
Box 6596
Huntington Beach, CA
92615
(800) 969-4417

PAPER SOURCE
232 West Chicago Ave.
Chicago, IL 60610
(312) 337-0798

Textile inks and supplies:

DHARMA TRADING CO.
Box 150 916
San Rafael, CA 94915
(800) 542-5227
In CA: (415) 456-7657

SCREEN PROCESS
SUPPLIES
530 MacDonald Ave.
Richmond, CA 94801
(510) 235-8330

Archival/ conservation materials:

CONSERVATION
RESOURCES
8000-H Forbes Place
Springfield, VA 22151
(800) 634-6932

ARCHIVART
7 Caesar Place
Moonarchie, NJ 07074
or Box 428
Woodridge, NJ 07075
(201) 804-8986

UNIVERSITY
PRODUCTS INC.
517 Main St. PO Box 101
Holyoke, MA 01041-0101
(800) 628-1912
In MA: (800) 336-4847)

LIGHT IMPRESSIONS
439 Monroe Ave.
Box 940
Rochester, NY 14603-0904
(800) 828-6216

LINECO, INC.
517 Main St.
Box 2604
Holyoke, MA 01041-2604
(800) 322-7775

appendix d:
herbarium collections and botanical gardens

There are herbarium collections of plant specimens all over the world, most of which serve as research institutions exclusively for the botanical community. Some are highly specialized, such as the Ross Potato Herbarium in Hamburg, Germany, or the Arizona State University Lichen Herbarium, in Tempe. Most herbariums were established as plant "libraries" for botanical gardens; and some have been in existence since the eighteenth century. Some of the larger institutions, like Kew, as noted below, have extensive Web pages that give full descriptions of botanical holdings, educational programs, and live plant collections. Many offer educational programs and services for the general public, for example, plant identification. Listings of hundreds of herbariums and natural history museums worldwide can be found on the internet at *http://www.helsinki.fi/kmus/botmenu.html* and through the Web site of the New York Botanical Garden, listed on page 155.

The following highly selective listing of herbariums and museums is intended to show the range and type of botanical information available to the general public.

The Botanical Garden of Padua, Italy

(*http://www.unesco.org/whc/sites/824.html*) Founded in 1545, this is the world's oldest botanical garden, although its sister institution at Pisa was established at almost the same time. Padua still preserves its original layout—a circular central plot (*hortus conclusus*), symbolic of the world, surrounded by a ring of water—and some of its sixteenth-century plantings are still in cultivation. During the eighteenth century, the gardens were embellished with fountains, ornamental entrances, statuary, masonry greenhouses, and also with more practical innovations such as pumping installations. Padua continues to be used as a botanical research institution with nearly six thousand plants cultivated on the site and a herbarium containing large numbers of rare specimens. It also has a seed exchange program with 693 botanical gardens around the world.

The Royal Botanic Gardens, Kew, England

Kew offers an eight-week course in Herbarium techniques every two years and runs regional courses in partnership with overseas institutions. The course textbook, *The Herbarium Handbook,* is available for sale through the Kew Shop.

The Natural History Museum, London

This museum's botanical web page has information about special programs and exhibitions and also displays an image of a herbarium specimen from the archives, together with a biography of the collector with whom it is identified.

The Jepson Herbarium, Berkeley, California

(http://ucjeps.berkeley.edu) Affiliated with the University of Southern California at Berkeley, this herbarium offers weekend workshops that range from courses in basic botany to field trips into the Mojave Desert. The herbarium is available by appointment and with statement of purpose to non-professionals.

The Field Museum of Natural History, Chicago, Illinois

In addition to extensive natural history exhibitions, this museum also maintains a collection of 2.6 million specimens, which is especially rich in flowering plants and ferns of the Americas. High school intern programs are offered as is university and postgraduate training in botany.

The Harvard University Herbaria / Botanical Museum, Cambridge, Massachusetts

This herbarium ranks eighth in the world in number of specimens—five million—and includes the once separate collections of the Arnold Arboretum, the Economic Herbarium of Oakes

Ames, the Oakes Ames Orchid Herbarium, the Farlow Herbarium, the Gray Herbarium, and the New England Botanical Club Herbarium. Ancillary collections include the world-famous Ware Collection of three thousand actual-sized glass models of plants that includes 840 species.

The New York Botanical Gardens, Bronx, New York *(http://www.nybg.org/bsci/ih/ih.html)* The NYBG houses one of the world's largest herbariums, which is accessible only to serious researchers. However the NYBG's library is open to the public and its catalog listings include thousands of horticultural and botanical texts and images. The NYBG is the site of an annual spring show and sale of garden antiques where one can usually purchase botanical specimens, botanical prints, antique herbaria, and books.

The Brooklyn Botanical Gardens, Brooklyn, New York *(www.bbg.org)* The Science Center of the BBG is conducting an ongoing survey of native and non-native plants in New York City. Called "Metropolitan Plants," the program welcomes the participation of amateur botanists who can help identify plants in specific mapped areas. The adult education department conducts plant pressing classes once a year.

The Marion Ownbey Herbarium, Pullman, Washington *(wsherb@mail.wsu.edu)* Part of Washington State University, this herbarium provides a variety of services to the public on plant identification, plant distribution, poisonous plants, weeds, and the human uses of plants. The herbarium also offers programs on local plants, taxonomy, and will consider special requests for group workshops and herbarium tours.

bibliography

Armstrong, Carol. *Scenes in a Library: Reading the Photograph in the Book, 1843–1875.* Cambridge, MA: October Books/The MIT Press, 1998.

Barber, Lynn. *The Heyday of Natural History, 1820–1870.* Garden City: Doubleday & Company, 1980.

Bethmann, Laura Donnelly. *Nature Printing with Herbs, Fruits & Flowers.* Pownal, VT: Storey Communications, Inc., 1996.

Blunt, Wilfrid. *The Art of Botanical Illustration.* London: Collins, 1967.

Bonta, Marcia Myers. *Women in the Field.* College Station, TX: Texas A & M University Press, 1991.

Bragshaw, Christopher. *Plant Collecting for the Amateur.* Victoria, Canada: Royal British Columbia Museum, 1996.

Brickell, Chris, Ed. *American Horticultural Society Encyclopedia of Garden Plants.* New York, NY: Macmillan/A DK Book, 1989.

Buckland, Gail. *Fox Talbot and the Invention of Photography.* Boston, MA: David R. Godine, 1980.

Carlson, Shawn. "Expert Secrets for Preserving Plants." *Scientific American,* June 1999.

Cave, Roderick and Geoffrey Wakeman. *Typographia Naturalis.* Wymondham, England: Brewhouse Press, 1967.

Coats, Alice M. *The Plant Hunters.* New York, NY: McGraw-Hill Book Company, 1970.

Danielsson, Bengt. *Gauguin in the South Seas.* New York, NY: Doubleday & Co., Inc., 1966

Desmond, Ray. *The History of the Royal Botanic Gardens, Kew.* Kew, Great Britain: The Harvill Press with the Royal Botanic Gardens, Kew, 1995.

Ewing, William A. *Flora Photographica: Masterpieces of Flower Photography 1835 to the Present.* New York, NY: Simon and Schuster, 1991.1

"Ferns and thier portraits," *The Quarterly Review,* No. 201, London: January, 1857.

Frizot, Michel, Ed. *A New History of Photography.* Koln, Germany: Konemann, English-language edition, 1998.

Gernsheim, Helmut & Alison. *A Concise History of Photography.* New York, NY: Grosset & Dunlap, 1965.

Greene, Edward Lee. *Landmarks of Botanical History,* 2 vols. Edited by Frank N. Egerton. Stanford, CA: Stanford University Press, 1983.

Harris, Elizabeth. *The Art of the Nature Print,.* exhibition catalog. Washington, DC: Smithsonian Institution, 1989.

Hawks, Ellison. *Pioneers of Plant Study.* New York, NY: Ayer Co. Publishing, 1928.

Healey, B. J. *The Plant Hunters.* New York, NY: Charles Scribner's Sons, 1975.

Heilmann, Peter N. Stephan Oettermann, and Armin Geus. *Natur im Druck.* Marburg, Germany: Basilisken-Presse, 1995.

_____. "Let's Talk a Little Bit About Nature Printing." Nature Printing Society Newsletter, June, 1995.

_____. (September, 1995).

_____. (December, 1995).

Hochberg, F. G. *Nature Printing: History and Techniques.* Melbourne, Australia: Museum of Victoria, Melbourne, 1985.

_____. "Impressions of Nature. Terra." Los Angeles, CA: The Natural History Museum of Los Angeles County, Vol 223, No. 1, Sept/Oct 1984.

Isley, Duane. *One Hundred and One Botanists.* Ames, IA: Iowa State University Press, 1994.

Keeney, Elizabeth, B. *The Botanizers.* Chapel Hill, North CA: The University of North Carolina Press, 1992.

Kraus, Hans P., *Sun Pictures: Photogenic Drawings by William Henry Fox Talbot.* Cat. 7. Text by Larry J. Schaaf. New York, NY: Hans P. Kraus, Jr. Fine Photographs, 1995.

Ladd, Henry. *The Victorian Morality of Art.* New York: NY: Octagon Books, 1968.

Mattenklott, Gert. *Karl Blossfeldt: The Alphabet of Plants.* Edited by Ann and Jurgen Wilde. New York, NY: te Neues Publishing Company, 1997.

Mayhall, Yolanda. *The Sumi-E Book.* New York, NY: Watson-Guptill Publications, 1989.

Moore, Randy, W. Dennis Clark, and Darrell S. Vodopich. *Botany,* 2nd Edition. New York, NY: WCB/McGraw-Hill, 1988.

Morewood, William. *Traveler in a Vanished Landscape: The Life & Times of David Douglas, Botanical Explorer.* New York, NY: Clarkson N. Potter, Inc., 1973.

Nature Printing Society, The. *The Art of Printing from Nature: A Guidebook.* Lake Shore, MN, 1997.

Newman, Eric. "Nature Printing on Colonial and Continental Currency," *The Numismatist,* February—May, 1964. American Numismatic Association, Colorado Springs, CO.

Parry, Eugenia. *Adam Fuss.* New York, NY: Arena Editons, 1997.

Pavord, Anna. *The Tulip.* New York, NY: Bloomsbury Publishing, 1999.

Peattie, Donald Culross. *Green Laurels: The Lives and Achievements of the Great Naturalists.* New York, NY: Simon and Schuster, 1939.

Philadelphia Museum of Art exhibition, May 2 to June 9, 1963: *A World of Flowers: Paintings & Prints.* Philadelphia Museum of Art Bulletin, Vol. LVII, No. 277 (Spring, 1963), pp. 236-242.

Philip Taaffe: Composite Nature, including "A Conversation with Stan Brakhage." November 15, 1997—January 31, 1998. New York, NY: Peter Blum Gallery, 1997.

Reveal, Thomas L. *Gentle Conquest: The Botanical Discovery of North America with Illustrations from the Library of Congress.* Washington, DC: Starwood Publishing, 1992.

Rosenblum, Naomi. *A World History of Photography.* New York, NY: Abbeville Press, 1984.

Rosenthal, Mark. *Anselm Kiefer.* Chicago: The Art Institute of Chicago, and Philadelphia: The Philadelphia Museum, 1987.

Rosenthal, Nan. *Anselm Kiefer: Works on Paper in the Metropolitan Museum of Art.* New York: NY: The Metropolitan Museum of Art/Harry N. Abrams, 1998.

Schaaf, Larry J. *Sun Gardens: Victorian Photographs by Anna Atkins.* Organized by Hans P. Kraus, Jr. New York, NY: Aperture Press, 1985.

Schama, Simon. *Landscape and Memory.* New York, NY: Vintage Books, 1996.

Scourse, Nicolette. *The Victorians and Their Flowers.* London, England: Croom Helm/Portland, OR: Timber Press, 1983.

Smith, Graham. *Disciples of Light: Photographs in the Brewster Album.* Malibu, CA: The J. Paul Getty Museum, 1990.

Stafleu, Frans A. *Linnaeus and the Linnaeans: The Spreading of their Ideas in Systematic Botany, 1735–1789.* Utrecht, Netherlands: Published by A. Oosthoek's Uitgeversmaatscapppij, N.V., for the International Association for Plant Taxonomy, 1971.

Watkins, T. H. "The Greening of the Empire," *National Geographic,* November, 1996, pages 28–52.

Wells, Diana. *100 Flowers and How They Got Their Names.* Chapel Hill, NC: Algonquin Books, 1997.

Whittle, Tyler. *The Plant Hunters.* New York, NY: Lyons & Burford, 1997.

index